D0616730

HEALTH-
WEALTH

9 STEPS TO FINANCIAL RECOVERY

IS HEALTHCARE BANKRUPTING YOUR BUSINESS?

HEALTH-WEALTH

9 STEPS TO FINANCIAL RECOVERY

DR. JOSH LUKE

ForbesBooks

Published by ForbesBooks, Charleston, South Carolina.
Member of Advantage Media Group.

ForbesBooks is a registered trademark, and the ForbesBooks colophon is a trademark of Forbes Media, LLC.

Printed in the United States of America.

10 9 8 7 6 5 4 3 2 1

ISBN: 978-1-946633-10-1
LCCN: 2017963439

Cover design by George Stevens.
Layout design by Megan Elger.

This publication is designed to provide accurate and authoritative information in regard to the subject matter covered. It is sold with the understanding that the publisher is not engaged in rendering legal, accounting, or other professional services. If legal advice or other expert assistance is required, the services of a competent professional person should be sought.

 Advantage Media Group is proud to be a part of the Tree Neutral® program. Tree Neutral offsets the number of trees consumed in the production and printing of this book by taking proactive steps such as planting trees in direct proportion to the number of trees used to print books. To learn more about Tree Neutral, please visit **www.treeneutral.com**.

Since 1917, the Forbes mission has remained constant. Global Champions of Entrepreneurial Capitalism. ForbesBooks exists to further that aim by bringing the Stories, Passion, and Knowledge of top thought leaders to the forefront. ForbesBooks brings you The Best in Business. To be considered for publication, please visit **www.forbesbooks.com**.

TABLE OF CONTENTS

PART I—HEALTHCARE IN AMERICA: CAPITALISM GONE WRONG

PART II—EMPLOYEE OWNERSHIP OF HEALTHCARE DECISIONS AND SPENDING

PART III — NINE STEPS TO CORPORATE HEALTH-WEALTH

ACKNOWLEDGMENTS

I WANT TO START by thanking my wife Martine for allowing me to be me … a writer, a futurist, a speaker, a podcast host, a social media influencer, a consultant, a strategist, an event host, and, most importantly, a husband and father. I wrote this book while also juggling three high-school-aged children. It's been a hectic few years but none of it would be possible without her.

I would also like to thank Dr. Anthony Slonim, CEO of Renown Health in Reno, Nevada, for writing the foreword and Dr. David Feinberg, CEO of Geisinger, for making his staff available to me.

I am grateful to the ForbesBooks team who was consistent and confident in their belief that I had the expertise needed to write this book on behalf of everyone who still believes in the American Dream. Thanks to everyone at Forbes, starting with Steve Forbes and including Justin Batt, Rusty Shelton, Adam Witty, and everyone who demanded my best at every stop!

Although I am sure to accidentally leave out a few people, I would like to thank the following individuals for sharing their expertise with me in preparing this book: Dawn Ahner, Cody Buhler, Dave Chase, Dr. Eric Coleman, Dr. Leigh Erin Connealy, Chad Fotheringham, Rudy Franco, Matthew Hanson, Mike Hartman, Kyle Hill, Tafa Jefferson, Richard Jung, Dr. David Ledbetter, Serrah Linares, Bill Massey, Ryan Miller, Diana Morris, Harry Nelson, Sunny Neogi, John O'Connell, Mike Ochoa, Katherine (Kat) Quinn, Jim Rossi, Dr. Tracy Smith, Yvonne Tanner, Ankur Teredesai, Mike Townsend, Jared Turner, Haley Hinman and the wardrobe team at David August for styling me out, and freelance photographer Marc Jay (on Instagram @marc.jay_) for taking the killer cover photos.

Thank you all for making this book a reality.

FOREWORD

I HAD THE GREAT FORTUNE of meeting Dr. Josh Luke several years ago. Over the intervening time, I have had the opportunity to become increasingly familiar with his work and thoughts on healthcare.

Josh has a progressive and innovative approach to solving some of the major challenges that confront our industry. Personally, as a cancer survivor, I have seen and experienced the inner workings of healthcare—some of it good, some of it not so good. For those of us who are drawn to healthcare because of our passion to help others, Josh continues to challenge us with better ways to deliver high quality, cost-effective care for the populations we are entrusted to serve.

It comes as no surprise to me that in his new book, *Health-Wealth: 9 Steps to Financial Recovery*, he is branching out beyond the healthcare industry. He is helping purchasers of healthcare understand the options available to them so that they can be better consumers.

In my work as a health system CEO, I have come to realize just how important our employees are and how their personal health directly affects our ability to serve the needs of our community. Healthcare in America is in crisis and, as CEOs, we have an obligation to assure that our employees get access to healthcare that is of the highest quality and lowest cost. In this book, Josh lays out a backdrop of the biggest healthcare issues we face as a nation. Accompanied by personal stories of his own, he reflects on the true magnitude of the healthcare crisis. Josh has engineered a series of steps that, when combined, create a manifesto that can address the challenges faced by companies large and small who are providing healthcare for their employees and their own families.

As a healthcare leader, I am encouraged by the challenges we have to confront. I believe that the more people who truly understand healthcare's challenges, the better off we will be to engage in discourse to improve our system of care.

In this book, Josh looks into the future so that we can all be optimistic about our role in changing healthcare for the better. Enjoy.

Anthony D. Slonim, MD, DrPH
President and CEO, Renown Health
Professor, Internal Medicine and Pediatrics
University of Nevada, Reno, School of Medicine

PREFACE

HEALTH-WEALTH: IS HEALTHCARE BANKRUPTING YOUR BUSINESS?

THE COST OF HEALTHCARE in America will continue to increase. It's a certainty. It's capitalism. Year after year, your company's health insurance carrier continues to increase your expenses—by at least 5 percent annually, on average. And while business owners and operators complain, many feel helpless and trapped, so they just keep their head in the sand and continue to pay.

There is a direct correlation between hyperinflating healthcare costs and deteriorating wealth in America. I am prepared to help you do something to keep healthcare from destroying your business— introducing *Health-Wealth*'s nine steps to financial recovery.

I am passionate about educating Americans on how to prevent Health-Wealth loss from destroying businesses. Health-Wealth is more than just a rhyme. In recent years, these two words have represented the antithesis of each other in American business. Businesses often can't have one (wealth) as a direct result of the other (overpriced *health*care). So as American businesses, in many ways we are being forced to choose between our employees' health and our organizations' wealth.

Well, choose no longer. Take control.

The intent of this book is not solely to place blame, but to break down the current healthcare delivery model and illustrate how it affects the reader and American businesses. The book will provide enhanced knowledge of current policies and their likely impact on businesses. Those companies that recognize the Health-Wealth corporate crisis bankrupting American businesses and that are first to adapt to new specialized programs will reap the financial benefits—and so will their employees and investors. This book is your handbook to end the annual premium increases and discover alternative approaches to improve the health of your employees. The result of you reading this book will be a healthier workforce, a happier workforce, and savings of more than 30 percent annually on overall healthcare spending for both your organization and its employees.

> *The result of you reading this book will be a healthier workforce, a happier workforce, and savings of more than 30 percent annually on overall healthcare spending for both your organization and its employees.*

Part I of this book describes the evolution of the American healthcare delivery model, to establish a basic understanding of why the delivery system is broken beyond repair and why, as a result, costs will continue to increase.

Part II of the book describes the growth of consumer-driven healthcare models, more commonly known as *high-deductible plans*, and how this model will continue to expand, as it has proven to be effective in increasing employee engagement in critical and expensive healthcare decisions.

Part III of the book explains nine simple, turn-key tactics companies can implement to save more than 30 percent annually on total healthcare spending.

Declare that your company has reached its tipping point. Commit yourself to leading your organization to improved employee health and significant corporate wealth. Your Health-Wealth journey begins here.

PART I

HEALTHCARE IN AMERICA: CAPITALISM GONE WRONG

CHAPTER I

THE AFFORDABILITY CRISIS

EAGER TO ATTACK the day on a Monday morning just three days before Thanksgiving 2004, I showed up for work a few minutes early to see if the hospital was entering the holiday week ahead of budget for the month. Six months earlier, just a few weeks after my thirty-second birthday in May 2004, I started in the role of Chief Executive Officer for Anaheim General Hospital.

My executive assistant, Cinthia, greeted me as usual, with a morning hello, and then inquired about my weekend. I loved holiday weeks as, although I was a workhorse always focused on measurable deliverables, I appreciated the slower pace of e-mails and calls during holiday weeks. They always provided some downtime. As I got settled into my cushy, leather executive chair, Cinthia walked in with an oversized manila envelope from corporate and handed it to me. As she turned and walked out, I stared in disbelief at the short but pointed handwritten note in the envelope.

It was a blank spreadsheet with a Post-It note on top. The Post-It simply said, "Great job increasing the total daily patient census. The boss wants to trim staff now. Fill out this list with forty names and their salary and return it by Friday. Thanks."

Silence. Disbelief. A pit in my stomach. Embarrassment. Despair. So many other emotions. How was this possible? We were growing in volume, and now we had to cut staff? And *forty* staff? Who would care for the patients?

At 8:31 a.m., the phone rang. It was my boss Mike, who reported to the corporate president. The conversation was short: "You're doing great, the hospital is way ahead of the projected turnaround plan, but the boss is testing you on this one. He is very happy with your performance to date. Keep it going. Get me that list by Friday."

Ten years in college, three degrees and a lot of hard work had led to what looked to be the opportunity of a lifetime. With three pre-elementary kids and a new mortgage, I was thrilled to be living in my hometown, pulling a six-digit salary with huge bonus potential, and on my way to a long career in hospital management. I had established a reputation in the healthcare space as a financial turnaround artist, having recently financially revived two nursing homes in a matter of months—not years, as was the norm—and six months earlier, I had been handed the microphone for the main stage: CEO.

> *On my way to a long career in hospital management, I had established a reputation in the healthcare space as a financial turnaround artist, having recently financially revived two nursing homes in a matter of months—not years, as was the norm.*

But to date, I had done it my way: turning around facilities through communication, transparency, fiscal responsibility, and treating employees and patients with respect and appreciation. This is why you get into health-care—to improve individuals' overall health. Until then, during my brief career in healthcare, I had never been put in a position where a financial decision forced upon me could potentially compromise patient care.

I had pursued a career in healthcare with a personal goal of making a difference in the lives of seniors. These layoffs were far from what I had imagined. Some tough decisions lay ahead, and yes, just before the holiday season. As my dad said once I got my first CEO gig, "This is why you get paid the big bucks."

> *To date, I had done it my way: turning around facilities through communication, transparency, fiscal responsibility, and treating employees and patients with respect and appreciation. This is why you get into healthcare—to improve individuals' overall health.*

The cost of operating a business in America will continue to increase. There is no doubt. Inflation, unions, cost of living, interest rate fluctuations, real estate costs, and healthcare coverage—it's your job to manage these expenses. Your company is counting on you.

In most companies, the most significant year-over-year expense increase in recent years has been the cost of providing health coverage to employees. The annual increases insurers require of American companies, whether mom-and-pop or Fortune 500, have been staggering for several years.

In fact, hundreds of companies have gone out of business in recent years simply because they did not foresee how healthcare was bankrupting their company. The writing was on the wall and had been for years, but they ignored it—*The Big Short*, healthcare version. *The Big Short* was a 2015 film that documented how, from 2005–2007 almost every industry and every individual in America chose to keep their head in the sand and ignore the inevitable, as subprime lending statistics demonstrated that a nationally devastating crash of the entire financial and real estate sectors was not only probable but inevitable. In 2007–2008, the United States experienced this crisis, which proved financially catastrophic to many businesses and bankrupted many families.

> *In most companies, the most significant year-over-year expense increase in recent years has been the cost of providing health coverage to employees.*

If only life had a rewind button. The next economic crisis and bankruptcy scare could be yours. You personally could be faced with that critical moment, where you are forced to decide between massive staff layoffs, filing for bankruptcy, going out of business, or laying off longtime, dedicated employees to cut costs. Are you prepared?

So let me be the first to ask you, as the keeper of your business: What are you going to do about it? The future success of your company is on your shoulders. Ever-increasing healthcare costs will bankrupt you if you allow it. Time is running out.

Your business's affordability crisis is America's affordability crisis. It's an American financial epidemic. It's no fault of yours that your company has inexplicably paid huge increases in recent years for health coverage, all while the insurer reduced the benefits afforded to you.

Well, there is one thing you can do. It's time for you to declare that your company has reached its "Health-Wealth tipping point."

In the hospital business, we have what we call "core staffing." This term simply refers to the bare minimum staff hospitals are legally required to have on hand at all times to care for patients. Hospitals go out of business when revenues no longer exceed the costs of core staffing on a consistent basis. That's capitalism 101.

So, what is your industry's "core staffing"? What's the phrase or term you use to describe that bare minimum of resources required to operate your company? At what point do your revenues no longer exceed your stripped-down, bare-minimum, can't-operate-without-these-items-in-place costs?

A critical next step as you begin your Health-Wealth journey is to identify your company's Health-Wealth opportunity. Once you identify your company's total, all-inclusive spending on healthcare in the prior fiscal year, there are three steps to identifying your Health-Wealth opportunity.

A. Project an increase of 6 percent a year for three years to identify your total spending amount on healthcare three years from now (X).

B. Subtract 20 percent from last year's annual spend to identify potential spending reduction (Y).

C. Health-Wealth opportunity = X – Y

or

Health-Wealth opportunity = (year 3 total) – (potential spending reduction from prior year)

Looking back now, I was clearly blindsided by this directive from my new boss shortly after becoming a CEO. As a young executive, I was confident and felt that my diverse career experiences to date had prepared for whatever would be thrown at me. Although I had rapid success in healthcare management in just a few short years, I fell into this career by accident. I'm just another Gen Xer from So Cal who grew up watching Bon Jovi and Michael Jackson on MTV, dreaming of hitting long balls for the Dodgers or dropping three pointers for the Showtime-era Lakers. Healthcare was the furthest thing from my mind as I went to college and then grad school.

So when I found myself sitting on a private jet in October 1998, flying to New York with the most famous baseball player in the world at the time, needless to say, I was content. Renowned baseball slugger Mark McGwire had just broken Major League Baseball's single-season home run record of sixty-one home runs in September 1998, and the global public relations firm I was working for was retained to handle his personal marketing efforts. I escorted Mark to interviews with *Time* magazine, who was considering him as a "Man of the Year" candidate, the Today Show, the Late Show with David Letterman, and the once-popular Rosie O'Donnell Show.

But then something unexpected happened. It was on the private jet back from New York that I found myself sharing with my wife for the first time that I was feeling unfulfilled in my career. After working with professional athletes in golf, basketball, baseball, football, and hockey for several years, I was losing my love for sports by working so closely with athletes, and I was now focused on raising a family.

My wife and I were living outside of California at the time, and my frequent calls home to Southern California to check on my aging grandmother's well-being often led to frustration. I was perplexed by how her caretakers at the hospital and in the nursing home had so little communication when she transferred from one facility to the other. I was even more shocked to find that when my grandma was transferred home from one of these facilities, the home-based caretakers seemed to have little instructional communication from the hospital or nursing home. This entire process made very little sense to me. I was beyond baffled; I was angry.

Anyone would be angry, right?

I made a career change and began learning the trade of healthcare administrator in a nursing home—a change that was inspired by my ailing grandmother. Just a few months after marketing NBA players and managing marketing efforts for a PGA Tour event, my focus had turned to caring for compromised seniors who lived within the walls of a nursing home.

It was baptism by fire—learning on the job came at me quickly. I also learned early on after the career change that margins were high for healthcare providers, doctors, and suppliers, because their costs were ultimately being passed on to patients and employers. There were integrity issues being exploited by business owners at every level of care. It was clear to me there was an absence of relevant checks and balances to keep spending under control.

In September 2017, Fierce Healthcare reported that the costs to employers to provide health insurance to its employees increased for a sixth straight year.[1] Well, that's why I am writing this book. You are one of the lucky ones who still have time to address the issue of the inexplicable annual increase in healthcare costs your company has been incurring in recent years. The revolution begins today.

"Forget Taxes, Warren Buffett Says. The Real Problem Is Health Care," was a recent *New York Times* headline after the share-holders meeting for Berkshire Hathaway in May 2017. Famed American financial icon and company CEO Warren Buffet stated that, about fifty years ago, "health care was 5 percent of G.D.P., and now it's about 17 percent." Buffet went on to state that "medical costs are the tapeworm of American economic competitiveness."[2] This pretty much sums up the problem.

How did we get here?

In the 1980s, the fee-for-service (FFS) approach and a standardized fee schedule were created to pay doctors for each of the different services they provide, both in hospitals and in their offices. So other than office visits, if a physician wants to increase his or her income, then patients must be sick and institutionalized in hospitals, nursing homes, or other post-acute institutions.

So what exactly is "fee-for-service"? According to Wikipedia (January 2017), FFS is a payment model where services are unbundled and paid for separately. FFS is the dominant physician payment method in the United States. In healthcare, it gives an incentive for physicians to provide more treatments, because compensation is dependent on the quantity of care rather than the quality of care. Similarly, when patients are shielded from paying (cost sharing) by health insurance coverage, they are incentivized to

---

1   Paige Minemyer, Fierce Healthcare, September 20, 2017.

2   Andrew Ross Sorkin, "Forget Taxes, Warren Buffett Says. The Real Problem Is Health Care," *New York Times*, May 8, 2017, https://www.nytimes.com/2017/05/08/business/dealbook/09dealbook-sorkin-warren-buffett.html.

welcome any medical service that might do some good. Thus, some of these "just to be safe" tests and treatments, ordered when insurance shoulders the majority of the costs, would be refused by the patient if the patient was responsible for the additional costs or a significant portion thereof.

I have a shorter, simpler answer for you. FFS is exactly what the name says. Your doctor gets paid a fee for providing you a service. Likewise, the hospital is paid a fee for providing you a service. If you are healthy and never need to go to a doctor or hospital for their services, then they don't get paid. Thus, the goal of doctors and hospitals is to put a head in a bed, so they can get paid—and then order as many tests as they can, so they can get paid.

> *If you are healthy and never need to go to a doctor or hospital for their services, then they don't get paid. Thus, the goal of doctors and hospitals is to put a head in a bed, so they can get paid—and then order as many tests as they can, so they can get paid.*

There are a number of problems with the FFS approach. The methodology, as described above, undoubtedly incentivizes and results in overutilization of services and delivery of expensive, unnecessary care. The FFS model financially incentivizes doctors to admit patients to hospitals and post-acute facilities and further rewards them financially for keeping patients in facilities for extended lengths of time. Not to mention the issue of primary care doctors taking care of their fellow physician buddies by referring often-unnecessary tests to them as specialists, which allows these specialists to bill for services as well.

While this is not the case for all physicians, of course, it is widely accepted and understood that this takes place in hospitals with a significant number of independent physicians who are not affiliated with or compensated by a larger group but rely strictly on the volume of patients seen daily for their income.

To be fair, it was not just doctors that were incentivized to institutionalize. Hospitals and post-acute facilities shared the same incentive. The FFS era drove the heads-in-beds strategy. That is how providers were reimbursed. This is also true for other inpatient providers, including nursing homes, long-term, acute-care hospital (LTACH), and acute rehab facilities have the same reimbursement methodology. The hospital or nursing home only benefits financially when a patient is admitted or receives care. Thus, the incentive is to find a reason—any reason—to admit a patient or order additional imaging or lab tests to identify potential concerns.

Are you looking forward to the day that you personally will be admitted to a convalescent home and told you will be living there for the remainder of your life? Most people chuckle when I make that statement. And that's fair. It's a laughable statement. Of course, no human being wants to be admitted to a skilled nursing facility (SNF). Perhaps some of our aging physicians should be reminded of this.

When you visit an emergency department, it is fair to assume that you are there to get evaluated by a medical doctor to see if care, medication, and treatment are necessary. But that assumption does not align with the reality of the business model of the hospital or the physician. Thus, the truth of the matter is that you are not there to be evaluated at all. By showing up to the emergency department, you are essentially volunteering to be a widget in a volume-based business model. For the past thirty years in America, we have referred to this as the FFS reimbursement model for doctors and hospitals.

Let's be clear about the business model. You are not in the emergency department to be assessed. You are in the emergency department so the doctor can identify a reason—in fact, any justification at all—to admit you to the hospital. Why? It's capitalism, and in American healthcare, a "head in a bed" is what drives profits for both hospitals and doctors. In the emergency room of American hospitals, you are a potential widget, and the doctors will run tests and order labs until they can identify a justification to convert you to a widget or, in more common terms, admit you to the hospital.

The key operational flaw in the FFS delivery model is that there is no required preauthorization for services. The term "managed care" emerged in the 1980s as a means to control this type of laissez-faire behavior by requiring the insurer to preauthorize any services ordered by a doctor or hospital. Without preauthorization, the doctor and provider do not get paid. There are many forms of managed care, but the one constant is a cost-control measure: written preauthorization from the insurer.

Without a required preauthorization, the delivery model was lawless, and much abuse took place. Fraud ran rampant in the healthcare sector as greedy hospital owners and physicians took advantage of an environment with no one at the helm. Thus, I have personally renamed the FFS era "the fee-for-service free-for-all."

In an era with explosive growth in the healthcare space, where there could not possibly have been enough oversight, the FFS era truly became a free-for-all, and it was lucrative for many. The problem was that the federal Medicare fund was disappearing at an alarming, unsustainable rate, and there was little evidence that this increase in spending was resulting in improved health or improved quality of care.

In FFS, there is a financial incentive for doctors and providers to order additional services—profit is based on quantity, not quality. It results in overutilization of services and delivery of expensive, unnecessary care. It incentivizes doctors to admit patients to hospitals and post-acute facilities and further rewards them financially for keeping patients in facilities for extended lengths of time. Patients often simply pay a minimal copay regardless of the volume of tests, and in turn patients are also incentivized to welcome any medical service that might do some good. There are no checks and balances in FFS. A physician's order for care was the ultimate judge and jury; there was no preauthorization required for admission to these levels of care.

The FFS free-for-all was lucrative for all. One program in particular that utilized the FFS reimbursement model was Medicare. Medicare is the federal insurance program for Americans over the age of sixty-five. In recent years, approximately 22 percent of all Medicare patients admitted to an acute hospital are subsequently transferred to an institutionalized level of post-acute care (nursing home, LTACH, or acute rehab hospital). Although on the surface one would assume a doctor would only send a patient from the hospital to another institution as a last resort, that is not always the case. One reason for such a high volume of patients being transferred from hospitals to post-acute institutions instead of being discharged home is that their doctor is incentivized financially to keep them institutionalized.

Think about it. Let's provide a hypothetical example of a sixty-five-year-old male. The man calls his longtime family doctor, and this is what takes place:

> *Patient calls doctor:* "*Hey, Doc, I fell a week ago, and my hip is still hurting. Should I come see you or go straight to an orthopedic specialist?*"

> *Family doctor responds:* "*Come see me first. I will let you know if you need to see a specialist.*" *(This is the first unnecessary step*

in the process, but now the primary care physician gets to bill the payer.)

Patient visits family doctor at his office. *Family doctor examines patient and refers patient to the hospital for labs and imaging tests. Family doctor bills payer for office visit.*

Patient goes to hospital for labs and imaging tests. *Hospital bills payer for services provided.*

Hospital calls family doctor with results. *The doctor's fishing expedition (to find any possible issue with the patient) pays off, as he finds some minor swelling and a possible minor hairline fracture in one image, both of which would likely have healed on their own and never been a concern of the patient.*

Family doctor refers patient to orthopedic specialist. *Orthopedic specialist says he only has office hours two days a week, so it's best to meet him at the hospital. Orthopedic specialist advises patient to go back to the hospital but to report to the emergency room and advise the nurse that the orthopedic specialist told him to come to the emergency department.*

Patient goes to emergency department. *Patient reports to the nurse his minor hip discomfort from a week-old injury and that the orthopedic specialist advised him to go to the emergency department. Nurse calls orthopedic specialist, who orders additional x-rays and an MRI but does not have time to come to the hospital until twelve hours later, as he has other priorities. Hospital bills payer for emergency services, MRI, and x-ray.*

Nurse calls orthopedic specialist. *Nurse advises orthopedic specialist that the images have been returned. Radiology doctor hired by* the hospital documents that there is a possible hairline fracture but is unsure. Radiologist bills payer for reading images.

Orthopedic specialist orders the patient admitted to the hospital for observation and requests that the family doctor or assigned hospital primary care doctor perform the initial required history and physical upon admission. Hospital doctor (hospitalist) does history and physical on patient, as the family doctor was unavailable to drive over to the hospital that night. Hospitalist is unable to find any pertinent information about the patient documented in the notes or chart, so hospitalist asks the emergency department nurse why the patient is there. Nurse reports, "He fell a week ago and has discomfort in his hip. There may be a hairline fracture. The orthopedic specialist thinks the patient may need hip surgery and wants to evaluate him as a precaution." The hospitalist, who thinks a different exam may be more effective than those images already taken, orders an additional image done and notices some lab results slightly out of range. The hospitalist then orders a consult by a cardiologist. The hospitalist bills the payer.

Orthopedic specialist finally arrives at the hospital. Orthopedic specialist examines the patient, who has been at the hospital for ten hours now, and does not see any need to keep the patient hospitalized any longer. He advises the patient to take Motrin but wants to hold off on discharging the patient until the cardiologist completes his consult. Orthopedic specialist bills the payer.

Cardiologist completes consult. Cardiologist consults patient, finds no reason for concern, and discharges the patient home after twelve hours in the hospital. The cardiologist and the hospital bill for services.

All because the patient had a sore hip and needed Motrin. Which either doctor could have diagnosed without running any tests, and just feeling the affected area and doing some motion and stretch assessments. Do you wonder now why the Medicare fund is running dry and insurers require preauthorization for services? What if the patient had simply gone to the orthopedic specialist's office first? The result would have been identical, as each of those tests was unnecessary. This practice still continues today.

The Patient Protection and Affordable Care Act (PPACA), also known as Obamacare, had a triple aim: improved care, better health, and lower cost (efficiency). President Obama's goal to reduce costs may have ultimately come to fruition, had Obamacare survived. But that savings was not going to manifest in this decade, even if Hillary Clinton was elected and Obamacare survived. Why? There were too many iterations, innovations, transitions, transformations, implementations, technological mandates, and leadership changes to get it all right so quickly.

So whether it's under Obamacare or some version of the Trump administration's tweaks to the delivery model, healthcare costs were destined to continue to increase for businesses and families either way after the 2016 election. But what gives? When do American businesses reach a Health-Wealth tipping point where they can no longer allow health insurers to increase rates annually for the same or fewer services? Well, that may be up to you.

It has been shown that at current pricing and income levels, it is expected that the millennial generation in the United States will spend an average of 40 percent of their lifetime earnings on healthcare. This is not practical. In fact, it's frightening. But at present, this is what the numbers show. America's affordability crisis is not just a crisis for your business but for your family as well. It's a healthcare affordability crisis on all levels—my family included.

In early 2011, the management company that owned the hospital I was running hired a new president who came in and made significant staffing cuts and sweeping leadership changes. Being one of the newer, younger executives, I was an easy target and found myself out of work for the first time since becoming a hospital CEO.

After six months of job-seeking, I received two job offers on the same day. My wife and I sat down with our children, discussed our options, and made the decision to leave California so I could manage a hospital in Las Vegas, Nevada. After less than a year in Nevada, though, we all missed Southern California and were anxious to move back. Once my employer caught wind of the fact that I was actively looking to return to Southern California, they abruptly ended my employment. Although I had been unemployed just a year earlier, I had been provided a severance package that covered our healthcare benefits the entire time between jobs, but this time around I was forced to decide whether to purchase health insurance for my family through COBRA.

Facing a move back to California and no job prospects, as my early departure was unanticipated, finances were tight. And when the COBRA invoice came in, the monthly premium was in excess of $1,300. Even though we had three children under the age of twelve at the time, this expense was hardly justifiable, even for your most precious assets—your children. We investigated other options, and even for the most basic benefit packages, we were looking at paying a minimum monthly premium in excess of $1,100—all while unemployed.

So in July 2012, my wife and I made one of the most difficult decisions of our lives: We decided to live without health insurance for ourselves and our children. It pains me to this day even thinking back on that decision. It was my own personal affordability crisis. It's as if no one in America can escape it. I had been a hospital CEO for almost eight years, with a great salary, and my family could not afford basic healthcare insurance. That's the moment I realized the American delivery system was broken beyond repair.

The reason we are facing this affordability crisis is capitalism. Everyone is trying to make a buck. And to date, many have succeeded! And it's not about Obama or Trump, or a Democratic or Republican majority in Washington, DC. It is about finding an affordable model that meets everyone's needs: a seemingly impossible task.

America's healthcare delivery system is a capitalist's dream, an unstoppable machine with excessive margins for businesses at all levels. So long as American businesses and families are willing to pay, the system will continue to spiral out of control. I got into this business to serve senior citizens and make a difference in people's lives. But it became apparent within a few short years that my personal mission was at odds with the delivery model, as capitalism had interfered long before I arrived on the scene.

Our country's affordability crisis became my family's crisis when we went without healthcare benefits for more than six months in 2012, and it was quickly becoming my personal career crisis. The hurtful truth was this: As a hospital executive, I was now as much a part of the problem as anyone else working in healthcare. I had been labeled as an up-and-comer in the hospital space with the skill set to continue this culture of greed for years to come.

The mass layoff I was directed to conduct made for a tough holiday season for me in 2004, but not nearly as tough as it was for the forty individuals I had to lay off just weeks before the holidays. That round of layoffs was the first of many more I was directed to oversee by hospital owners and operators in my ten years as a hospital CEO. It was never an easy task to fire someone when they knew business was improving. My job as CEO was to motivate employees and tell our story of success each day, so it was understandable when individuals being fired were in disbelief when they learned that the company was laying off forty employees, effective immediately. Balancing corporate greed without compromising patient care became more and more difficult with each year that passed. The effect of that greed is increased costs passed on to American businesses and families.

This culture of greed has bankrupted hundreds of once-thriving American businesses. It will bankrupt many more in coming years. Will your business be the next victim of this culture of greed? That may be up to you.

CHAPTER 2

A CULTURE OF GREED

IN 2014 I WAS ASKED to serve as CEO of an inner-city hospital in Los Angeles. As CEO, I would "round the hospital floors" daily, greeting staff, patients, and guests. I recall walking into a patient room on the medical-surgical unit one morning only to be approached by two middle-aged men. Their body language and facial expressions exuded frustration as I reached my hand out to introduce myself as the hospital CEO.

"Does our mother have to go to this other hospital the doctor keeps mentioning?" one of the brothers asked, as their aging mother edged to the side of her hospital bed to stand up.

"And how come the doctor is making me stay two more days when I told him I was fine and the nurse said I was cleared to go as well?" the patient asked.

Although it would have been appropriate to discharge the patient home that day, the doctor had other plans: plans rooted in greed. By keeping the patient in the hospital two more days, even if she did not need to be hospitalized, the doctor would make an additional $110. And instead of discharging her to recover and heal at home, the doctor was documenting that the patient could benefit from an LTACH stay. The average length of stay in an LTACH is twenty-five days, and the referring doctor is reimbursed daily. So whether she needed it or not, their mom was going to be institutionalized for another twenty-seven days, all for the sole reason that the doctor viewed her as a widget that produced income for him.

I encouraged the two brothers and the patient to chat with the doctor and advised them that they were free to disagree with the doctor at any time and go home.

To further explain, Medicare reimburses doctors $55 a day on average for a routine hospital visit. Medicare Guidelines have a baseline length of stay for each patient diagnosis. Patients with their mom's diagnosis had a mean length of stay of five days, even though she had only been in the hospital three days so far.

The doctor was also being paid a monthly stipend by multiple LTACH hospitals and nursing homes to serve as their medical director. While the medical director has a list of monthly responsibilities, for the most part the nursing home or LTACH could live without them. The reality is that these agreements are in place so the facility can pay approximately $2,500–$5,000 a month to the doctor and in turn benefit from the revenue generated by the doctor sending the bulk of his or her patients to that facility (putting heads in their beds). Thus, there was even more incentive for the doctor to prioritize his own interest well above that of the patient.

Now imagine if this were your mother, or even a key employee who was being told they could not go back to work for almost a month, because they needed to be institutionalized. In fact, if it was your employee, it's a double whammy financially, as you are footing the expensive inpatient post-acute care, as well as missing their productivity in the workplace.

Capitalism. It's everywhere you look in healthcare, and it's bankrupting America, destroying the American dream—your American dream. Your business, your employees, and your family are the victims of healthcare's villains' greed. This chapter will detail the role each of these villains plays in making healthcare unaffordable and therefore inaccessible for many Americans—even middle-class, working Americans. The corporate villains passing these expenses on to your business and family include hospitals, insurers, insurance brokers, pharmaceutical companies, device manufacturers, and electronic medical record (EMR) companies, among others.

As already illustrated in the prior story, doctors in particular are incentivized to overprescribe and institutionalize. The FFS model incentivizes doctors to admit patients to hospitals and post-acute facilities and further rewards them for keeping patients in facilities for extended lengths of time. There are a number of problems with the FFS approach. The methodology, as described previously, undoubtedly incentivizes and results in overutilization of services and delivery of expensive, unnecessary care—the heads-in-beds strategy discussed earlier. Hospitals and post-acute facilities shared the same incentive.

There is one other component of FFS that completely changed how the doctor approached inpatient care. FFS reimburses a doctor for consulting a patient every day in an acute hospital, an LTACH, or an acute rehabilitation hospital, but not in a nursing home; the doctor can only bill for services once or twice monthly, in most cases. Additionally, in-home health doctors are permitted to bill even less than once a month. This one is the game changer. Let me explain.

The more patients a doctor transfers from the acute hospital to an LTACH or inpatient rehabilitation facility (IRF), the more personal income that physician can earn. Once doctors figured out they could bill for services daily in each of these settings, their tactics changed, and they started finding opportunities to justify additional patients going to each of these settings where they could can bill for services daily. It was prevalent during the fee-for-service era and led to significant wasteful spending of Medicare dollars. Welcome to the world of the "quota-based physician."

Quota-based physicianing became so entrenched in some doctors' daily routine that it became the norm. They would look for any justification they could to send a patient from the hospital to an LTACH or acute rehabilitation hospital simply so they could continue to bill for services daily.

So instead of considering sending the patient home as an option for discharge after a patient is hospitalized, active doctors who focused on caring for senior citizens became entrenched in a culture that they argued was based on "limited physician liability" by erring on the side of caution and sending patients to institutions after the hospital instead of to their homes. "I cannot send this patient home, as I'm liable if they fall and get hurt once they get home," a doctor might say. Those are pretty powerful words. They are certainly words that anyone who is not a physician is slow to challenge. The word *liability* usually ends the conversation, as no one would challenge the physician. It is the same word emergency room doctors use to justify admitting patients to the hospital as opposed to discharging them home from the emergency department—another example of wasted Medicare dollars in the FFS era.

The financial incentive for doctors to practice on a quota basis is significant. Doctors are taught these financially lucrative tactics by the very specialty hospitals that doctors refer patients to. These specialty hospitals, LTACHs, and acute rehab hospitals pay them a monthly stipend for providing allegedly "necessary" physician advisor quality assurance and support services. Many of these services have been legally challenged as unnecessary. When one of these services contracts expires (usually annually), the service agreement will not likely be renewed if the doctor had not been referring a significant volume of patients to the LTACH or IRF. Guess what? Once those "services" are no longer performed, there is no noticeable impact on the facility, its operations, its quality, or its patient satisfaction. So I ask you, if the services are "needed" to justify them legally, why is it that when they are no longer performed, no one misses a beat? It is all a sham, that's why.

How lucrative are the financial rewards of employing a quota-based approach for an independently practicing physician? An active doctor who has an average of ten patients a day in various acute hospitals who sends most patients home upon discharge unless they absolutely need to rehabilitate at an SNF, would receive reimbursement from Medicare of just under $279,000 annually. However, if that same doctor instituted a quota-based approach and found a justification to transfer as many of those patients as possible to an LTACH or acute rehab, he would receive approximately $672,000 annually in Medicare reimbursement. That is more than double the income. Sounds like a perfect material for a future episode of *American Greed*! These costs for often completely unnecessary post-acute stays are passed onto you the employer and to your family.

Quota-based physicians are also notorious for having an acute hospital length of stay that is longer than the norm. The reason they do this is, as always, financially motivated. Even though the patient may be healthy enough to go home after being in the hospital for three days, the physician is often able to collect one to two more days of reimbursement if the patient stays in the hospital. As awful as it sounds, your doctor could leave you in a hospital unnecessarily so he or she can collect an additional $55 in reimbursement. Welcome to the FFS American healthcare delivery model.

I operated and consulted for several hospitals where case managers and discharge planners reported examples of overly long hospital stays taking place regularly. It is downright awful. Even worse is that cash-strapped hospitals serving the inner city are often helpless to change the doctor's behavior, even when they have egregious examples. These hospitals are so desperate to put heads in beds that they are not about to bite the hand that feeds them by alienating a high-volume-referring physician. It would be career suicide for any hospital CEO to do so. Even though it's an almost inhumane practice, the hospital is helpless in many cases to address it.

As it relates to documentation, physicians can essentially justify anything they desire as long as they have a game plan from the start. Physicians know which tests to order to create a logical path to suggesting someone needs an LTACH visit after the hospital. Even in the absence of any justification, the mere fact that physicians are considered experts, along with their ability to document in a way that furthers their own goals instead of documenting the true facts, is enough reason for everyone to look the other way in the FFS era. I call this "documenting toward the discharge." It runs rampant in hospitals and post-acute facilities, where nurses and administrators often feel helpless to question a doctor's judgement, and it is a means for a doctor to paint a picture suggesting post-acute care is needed by simply knowing which words to write in a chart.

In addition to a lack of transparency on pricing, many leading hospitals are not-for-profit entities, meaning they are exempt from paying taxes. These hospitals are also required to create a community benefit plan each year to ensure specific community needs are being met. By allowing hospitals to maintain their not-for-profit status, it allows them to become dominant players and reduces the competitive landscape.

For example, if there is a local physician group that sends their high-reimbursement surgeries to a competing hospital, a hypothetical not-for-profit, in many cases, would just go offer to buy the entire physician practice, in turn ensuring that all the surgeries were referred to it. While a for-profit hospital could employ the same approach, there is not a level playing field, as the for-profit is subject to paying a signifi-cant amount of taxes each year. While hospitals maintaining not-for-profit status seems to be a hot topic in the media in recent years, there has been little action by individual states to address this issue.

Doctors who are employed or are part of a medical group have less incentive to operate in this manner, as they receive a salary in many cases. There are, however, quite a few doctors who prefer to remain independent so that they can practice as individual business owners. As a result, independent practice doctors have much more incentive to bill as many patients as possible and order as many tests as possible.

Let's think back to Chapter 1, where we clarified that emergency room doctors' true intent in the FFS era was not to evaluate you but simply to find a justification—any justification—to admit you to the hospital. The hospital is structured so that it contracts with physician groups for multiple services. Some of these services include emergency department, psychiatric, and others we will discuss later in the book. The point to be made here is that these physicians and physician groups are selected through a competitive bidding process. Ultimately, the hospital will select the group that proves to be the most financially lucrative, meaning the group that is most willing to be as aggressive as possible in putting heads in beds to drive revenue for all.

Just as described with the doctor in the emergency room finding justification to admit as many patients as possible, how do you think the hospital's psychiatrist reacts when the hospital calls, seeking a consultation for a patient who may have a psychiatric need? Let me state the obvious here: the hospital is not calling because the patient does *not* need a consult. Translation: the fact that a primary care doctor or nurse requested a psychiatric consult is traditionally all of the justification a hospital needs to keep a patient hospitalized for days and order a full slate of expensive psychotropic medications for the patient.

Thus, of course, anytime the hospital saw an opportunity to order a psychiatric consult, it was quick to react and encourage the doctor to write the order whether it was simply confusion, depression, stress, or anything else they could think of, including anxiety. A quick side note here: who doesn't have some anxiety when they are admitted to the hospital? It's a normal human characteristic to be stressed out and have anxiety when you are admitted to a hospital! I am an advocate for the behavioral health community, a board member for Alzheimer's organizations, and a former CEO of the largest acute psychiatric hospital in Orange County, California. As much as it pains me to share the above information with you, it's the cold-hearted truth of how hospitals maximize revenue. They seek to diagnose psychiatric issues even when they are not present or the reason for the hospital visit.

Almost every contracted service in the hospital structure was selected through a competitive bidding process. The hospital structure was such that the more methods to justify putting a head in a bed to drive revenue, the more lucrative it was for all. As a result, the FFS era truly became a free-for-all, as there were few checks and balances to control the over-prescribing and admitting of Medicare patients. If the doctor said the patient needed it, the patient got it, and the doctor and the hospital billed the federal government for services.

This lack of checks and balances for Medicare led to the rise of managed care products and ultimately to managed Medicare products like Medicare Advantage. Managed care is the opposite of FFS, as there are checks and balances at every step of the way. In fact, these checks and balances must be approved prior to receiving care, even with a physician order. This process is called *preauthorization* and is common for all health maintenance organization (HMO) product lines. While preferred provider organization (PPO) insurance products often allow the patient to seek primary care without preauthorization, even PPO products in many cases now require a preauthorization for specialized services as well. Both HMO and PPO products routinely offer a "narrow network" of hospitals to clients, which means the insurer and the patient pay less if the patient chooses one of the included hospitals.

But can we pause for a second and ask an obvious question at this point in the book? Why all the middlemen in healthcare? In fact, should we be asking if the insurance company is even necessary? I say, "Yes, we should definitely be asking!" One of the inherent issues with personal healthcare costs is that the health insurance industry is one of the few industries in the country that has a third party negotiating an individual's costs.

Think about it, you don't have a third party with you at the car dealership when negotiating a car price. You negotiate directly. Negotiation is not just an art that requires intelligence; it is a very emotional process as well. When you go to Walmart or Target, do you bring a third party with you to negotiate prices? No. But when necessary, you exercise the ultimate negotiating tactic and walk away when a store increases its prices to a level you are not comfortable with. So when will you, as the steward of your corporation, exercise the ultimate negotiation tactic and simply walk away from your health insurance partner?

Have you seen the annual compensation packages of managed care executives and health system executives? They are not poor. Several insurance CEO's take home more than $10 million in one year. I bet that's not the insurer's first message point on the agenda at the annual member town hall meeting! It might be the member's first agenda item, though! Imagine if that $17 million were split up among its members in the form of a rebate check or care credit? That could be a few bucks per member at a minimum. Kaiser Permanente, for example, earned $1 billion in operating gain in first quarter 2017. But their average client can barely afford their policy, if they can at all. And Kaiser is actually one of the more affordable options!

While I am all for capitalism and the free market, at some point, some of these few, very fortunate executives need to get a little closer to reality and understand how that message feels to a member who is struggling, or to a business executive like yourself who is negotiating rates. And this goes for health system executives as well. Everyone is entitled to make a living, and yes, there is great responsibility in these roles, but there are other benefits that can be offered other than simply compensation that assist in protecting an individual from liability. The federal government should be applauded for attempting to include safeguards in the PPACA to limit the spending and compensation of insurers, but it's a task that was much easier said than done.

Any way you look at it, some of the executive compensation packages in healthcare do not feel good to the struggling single mom or middle-class parents just trying to raise a healthy family. And I can't help but notice that each time I take my family to a Lakers game or Yankees game, the largest advertising banners in the arena and stadium are often occupied by insurance companies or not-for-profit hospitals. While Americans struggle to find the finances to access basic healthcare services, executives from insurers and hospitals are paying six to seven figures a year to wine-and-dine at the ball game in a luxury suite. In fact, at least six health systems nationwide spent more than $1.2 million on television ads alone in 2016, but most of those health systems' clients are likely unable to justify the amount of money spent on accessing healthcare. So I ask you, considering our healthcare affordability crisis in America, is this capitalism gone wrong?

Another area of concern that led to America's healthcare affordability crisis is the compensation packages of insurance brokers cutting deals with businesses. These brokers are often reimbursed on a per-enrollee basis, and their commission is often hidden in the fine print of the deals signed with corporate executives.

The broker relationship is a tricky one for a company, when you think about it. You can choose any broker you prefer, and the minute you do, they are trying to hide fees and commissions from you. The fact that their commission is greater with one insurer than the other may lead them to persuade you to choose an inferior insurer as well.

Brokers also include significant unjustified annual increases hidden in the fine print. So the guy you contract with to get you the best deal, who promises you over a steak dinner or in a luxury suite at the ball game that he or she will get you the best deal available, is often charging you more for services than the carrier is actually paying the provider.

So we have already discussed several of the obvious culprits in this greed game that led to the affordability crisis, including doctors, hospitals, insurers, and insurance brokers. Over the next few paragraphs we will discuss some of the less obvious culprits contributing to America's healthcare affordability crisis, including pharmaceutical companies, device manufacturers, and EMR companies.

Pharmaceutical companies represent another area of skyrocketing prices affecting consumers' ability to afford healthcare. The pharmaceutical industry has always pointed at the Food and Drug Administration's tedious process for bringing a new drug to market as its go-to reason for unjustifiably high pricing. If each new drug patent has a sixteen year window for exclusivity before other similar generic products can be brought to market, and the approval process takes, on average, eleven years, then the industry battle cry has always been "we can charge whatever we want for the remaining five or six years before generic versions hit the market." While there is truth to this reasoning, the antics and strategies employed by some manufacturers in increasing drug costs in recent years have been egregious at times and are a significant contributor to the healthcare affordability crisis in America.

Device manufacturers are no exception. Doctors have a choice of which hardware or device brand they use when operating on a patient or completing a procedure. The margins on many devices are, again, unjustifiable. It's often times just a plastic device, cheap to produce but expensive for the hospital to buy. While hospitals and insurers would prefer that the doctor use the most affordable product, doctors often go with the most expensive version. Why? Whether or not they think a specific product is the most effective, doctors are often compensated by device manufacturers as a means to ensure loyalty. This is very similar to the approach used by nursing homes and LTACHs to contract with doctors as medical directors to ensure referrals. Not surprisingly, this tactic has also been employed by pharmaceutical companies to ensure that doctors write prescriptions for their name-brand products.

Let me give you one example of why healthcare has grown so unaffordable to the average American. There are so many middlemen in healthcare that it is difficult to keep up. These middlemen are all pulling a profit, in most cases at a sizable margin. Look at supplies, for example. In order to adequately care for a patient, the supply process may go like this:

Manufacturer acquires raw materials	Hard cost
Manufacturer creates product/device	Hard cost
Manufacturer sells wholesale to medical supplier/distributor	Hard cost
Distributor secures delivery from trucking company	Hard cost
Hospital pays materials management staff to inventory	Salary
Central supply stocks hospital/operating room shelf	Salary
Nurse/physician administer product	Salary
Many devices require a manufacturer's trained rep in the room	Hard cost
Physician bills for application	Insurer billed
Hospital bills insurer for product and application of product	Insurer billed to cover all

Those are the ten steps to get a device to a patient. Each comes with a cost. That cost is ultimately passed on to your business, your employees, and your family.

EMR companies are another major contributor to the affordability crisis. When the PPACA was passed, it passed a series of requirements for hospitals and physicians to implement software and EMR on a short timeline. Do you think that led to lower prices and increased competition? Of course not! It led to price gouging, monopolistic tactics, excessive data blocking, and arrogant, deceptive, and misleading business practices from the leading EMR companies. Why? Because they could.

Within a few short months after Obamacare was passed, several big EMR companies were turning away small and medium-size hospitals as the "account was not big enough to bother with unless you are part of a larger health system." While change may bring opportunity, it did not guarantee innovation or progress in a timely manner when it came to technology, and costs for care shot through the roof as a result. Again, these costs are passed on by hospitals and doctors to businesses and families. All in the name of capitalism!

These things may seem far-reaching until you consider an episode of care that affected you personally. For example, I lived through an episode with my late grandmother during the last year of her life that exemplified so many of these examples contributing to the healthcare affordability crisis. In the summer of 2001, my grandmother Belva's congestive heart failure was progressing, so she ended up in the hospital. As discussed earlier, both the doctor and the provider (the hospital in this case) got paid for her care during the stay. Rather than ask her if she felt strong enough to go home, as home-based support services were available, the doctor placed his own personal financial interests ahead of my grandmother's preferences and advised her that she needed to be "transferred" to an LTACH to continue her recovery.

Doctors are very skilled at using terms like "transfer" instead of "discharge," as "discharge" may suggest the patient has a choice in the matter. The truth is, the patient always has a choice in the matter. But for some reason in America, patients are either not aware of that fact or are afraid to speak up.

When my grandmother arrived at the LTACH, she was surprised to learn that she would be staying for more than three weeks. Needless to say, she was disappointed. As was I—she appeared to me to be healthy enough to go home. But remember, both the doctor and the provider get paid at this stop, too. The "wink-and-nod" between the post-acute provider and the doctor is that monthly stipends are paid to the doctor, and in return, the doctor refers as many patients as possible so that the beds remain full. This clearly clouds the doctor's ability to provide unbiased input to patients in the hospital, as there is significant pressure to keep post-acute beds full.

After three weeks and four days in the LTACH, my grandmother was advised that she needed to continue her care in a "rehab facility." It should be no surprise to anyone that my grandmother stayed exactly twenty-five days, as twenty-five days is the average length of stay required to maximize Medicare reimbursement and maintain licensure for LTACHs. The bigger providers got so good at managing this length of stay within an average range of twenty-four to twenty-six days that the *Wall Street Journal* documented the egregiousness of this financially driven practice, which could not be linked to any sort of improvement in quality of care.[3]

---

3   Christopher Weaver, Anna Wilde Mathews, and Tom McGinty, "Hospital Discharges Rise at Lucrative Times," *Wall Street Journal*, Feb 17, 2015, http://www. wsj.com/articles/hospital-discharges-rise-at-lucrative-times-1424230201.

So after four weeks away from home in two different hospital settings, my grandmother reacted to the news of a "transfer" away from the LTACH by stating, "I thought I was rehabbing here. What is a rehab facility?" The reality is, it's a fancy name for a convalescent home or a nursing home. In fact, the long-term care industry has gone to great lengths in recent years to shed both of those names, replacing them with names such as SNF, short-term rehab, and express rehab facilities. There are two reasons for that:

1. Nursing home reimbursement for short-term therapy days ($300–$700) is two to four times greater per day than the reimbursement operators receive for long-term custodial patients who are unable to live at home any longer ($150–$200).

2. As stated earlier, no one wants to go to a convalescent home (or nursing home). In fact, many years ago, Baby Boomers promised their parents or grandparents that they would never make the decision to send their parents to a nursing home. As a result, the industry changed the name in the 1980's to 'nursing home' with the hope that patients in the hospital and their family members would not realize their loved one is actually going to a convalescent home (when in fact they are the same thing). Fast forward another generation and now you see the name "nursing home" losing favor for the same reason, and nursing homes are often being referred to as rehab facilities for the same reason! Its industry-calculated changing semantics!

Once she arrived at the convalescent home—I mean, skilled nursing facility (SNF)—both the doctor and the provider (SNF) got paid at this stop as well. Now you might be asking, how long does this go on before Grandma Belva gets to go home? Great question. The answer to that question should be the same whether she is in a hospital, doctor's office, LTACH, or SNF. The question is, more precisely, "Is Grandma Belva able to return home safely, and if so, what resources might she require in the home to ensure she will be safe to recover and rehabilitate?" During the FFS era, doctors rarely asked that question, as it would not have been as financially beneficial to them. In fact, each time my grandmother got passed to a different level of care, the financial incentives changed and, in a sense, started all over again for both the new provider and the doctor.

So once Grandma Belva was transferred to an SNF (frankly because she was led by her physician to feel that she did not have a choice in the matter), the very sweet social worker at the SNF advised her that they were hopeful she could heal fast enough to return home after three weeks. Three weeks! Why three weeks? Well, you are getting keen on how the system worked at this point. The longer a patient stays and participates in therapy, the more reimbursement the SNF receives at the lucrative rehab rates. Most patients plateau and no longer show rehab improvement between the tenth and seventeenth day in an SNF. Thus, SNFs try to maximize reimbursement by pacing the patient at a twenty-day rate to lengthen the projected stay and maximize the SNF's reimbursement. By goal-setting for twenty days you can often get the optimal outcome of 17-20 days of therapy.

And let us not forget the two financial incentives for physicians to refer patients to the SNF. They are identical to the two incentives in LTACH: Not only does the doctor get paid again for consulting the patient in a new SNF, but the doctor often collects a monthly stipend ($1,000–$4,000) from the SNF as well.

Again, this monthly stipend is often part of a sham, a handshake agreement allegedly in place for the doctor to perform "needed services" for the SNF, when in actuality, the understanding is that the doctor will refer a high volume of patients and keep the SNF's beds full. Needless to say, at the SNF level, just as other levels of care, both the doctor and the provider bill for services.

Finally, after three weeks in the SNF, my grandmother was miraculously finally ready to return home. However, the doctor advised her that unless she was willing to participate in home health therapy services, she would have to reside in the nursing home for the rest of her life. Wow! What a way to package two options for a senior to choose from. Door number one, please! "I will go home with home health services," she said. And yes, you guessed it, not only does the doctor get a monthly stipend from the home health agency (to refer patients, of course), but the provider and the physician once again billed the insurer.

It's the FFS free-for-all, no doubt about it. And if you were listening very carefully back in Southern California in the summer of 2002 you may have heard a collective cheer from the provider and physician community when my grandmother fell and was rushed back to the emergency room. Yep, it was time to put her back on the forty-five-day merry-go-round and let all the providers and doctors bill for delivering services to her. Imagine a world where providers and physicians actually just met her basic needs and comforted her emotionally so she could return home safely to age and heal in her own environment. The illustration below illustrates this service-driven model.

GRANDMA BELVA—CONGESTIVE HEART FAILURE

The Summer of 2002: Estimated Medicare Dollars Paid to Providers (Does Not Include Doctor)

Home	$0
Hospital	$48,000
LTACH	$52,000
Nursing home	$12,000
Home with home health	$4,000
Hospital	$36,000
Nursing home	$18,000
Assisted living with home health	$4,000
Hospital	$42,000
Nursing home	$24,000
Hospital	$58,000
Total costs of care	**$298,000**

The irony of this summer, and the accompanying graphic, is that my grandmother should have been placed on hospice months before her life ended, not weeks or days. The reality was that hospice services were obviously the next step in the process of her care for the final nine months of her life. But guess what? When doctors order hospice, the unlimited gravy train of billing for services for primary care doctors, specialists, and providers dries up.

Providers and physicians don't get paid when patients are healthy, so patients are often institutionalized unnecessarily for financial gain—whether willfully or not. It's likewise for when hospice is ordered. A few services can still be provided by doctors, but other than the hospice company and the medical equipment provider, the unlimited path of unaccountable billing for services for multiple parties dries up forever (in regard to that patient). It is very likely that home-based services could have been offered and could have improved her care while at the same time saving significant Medicare dollars. Guess what else? My grandmother would have been much happier being cared for in her home than at those different facilities. The problem? No one ever advised her that home-based care was an option. Why would they—it was not in their best interest.

So what is the physician's role in this scenario? Physicians are partners in crime in the specialty hospital incentivizing experiment—doctors who "shifted to the dark side" in a model that proved to be extremely lucrative for all. These doctors who abandoned the Hippocratic Oath in favor of capitalistic greed shared in the financial windfall of the model just as much as the specialty hospital owners and CEOs, who were pulling in $3–11 million annual compensation packages at times. And one last point: while technically legal in principle, at the very minimum, what is described in this chapter is not patient-centric and is, in many cases, beyond unethical. The doctors have learned what needs to be documented, and therefore abuse is difficult to prevent.

I share this story with you because so many of the factors contributing to the healthcare affordability crisis in America were exemplified by my grandmother's care plan. Quota-based physicianing exemplifies a number of the villains we showcased in this chapter, from doctors to multiple providers. Multiple devices were implemented in my grandmother's plan of care, and undoubtedly both she and the Medicare fund paid more than was necessary for medications throughout the process.

Let's be clear here on how these things contributed to the affordability crisis: aside from a few copayments paid by my family, all of my grandmother's costs for care (much of it unnecessary) were passed on to you! These costs are passed on to American businesses and taxpayers. When the Medicare fund runs dry, who replenishes the needed dollars? Taxpayers—American businesses, and families.

The handwritten letter my grandmother penned after returning home from the hospital near the end of that episode still resonates with me today. The letter said, "I am anxious to return home next week, four months is a long time to be away from home."

CHAPTER 3

A SYSTEM BROKEN BEYOND REPAIR

IN THE FALL OF 2016, my middle son was a freshman in high school and was in the thick of his first year of high school football. One night he came into my room after bedtime complaining of stomach pain. He was clearly in pain for an extended period of time, and because he had just gone through a full-contact high school football season, we were overly sensitive to any health issues he brought up. We made the decision to take him to the nearby emergency room.

The hospital is owned by a nationally known, for-profit chain with a well-publicized, checkered history of transparency. I knew the hospital well, as I had grown up in the area, I had been a patient in the emergency department myself in prior years, and my daughter had been born at the hospital. In fact, a few months earlier, their regional medical director contacted me to ask if I would interview for the hospital's vacant CEO position. It was a reputable, local community hospital.

After three hours in the emergency department and a number of tests to determine stomach pain, they told us that my son was fine. His pain had subsided, and they found no issues. Great, I thought. All's well that ends well.

Three weeks later, several bills arrived in the mail. I was not worried, as my family had a great PPO insurance plan, and this hospital was a contracted provider. I reviewed the bills, and total charges from the hospital alone were $19,908. My responsibility for the hospital component was $3,516. I was even put off at how much my insurance company paid: $7,970. All for three hours in the emergency room and a few tests. And I was also on the hook for the physician component of more than $1,080. The total costs to have my son's stomach ache assessed for less than three hours were almost $4,600 (see graphic on next page).

Maybe they should make this into an ad campaign, I thought. Instead of saying "The wait in our emergency room is less than fifteen minutes!" as is the norm for hospital advertising nationwide, perhaps they should consider a new campaign: "If you have a great PPO insurance policy, come to our emergency room and we only charge you $5,000!" What a deal!

Having been a hospital CEO, I have been on both sides of this issue. But in this moment, I was asking myself, did we consent to this? Did anyone tell us how expensive it was? So I called and requested a detailed invoice of expenses. A few weeks later, the detailed description of my son's three hours in the emergency room arrived in the mail.

It might as well have been a poster advertising the income opportunity for doctors and hospitals in the FFS era. The total charges exceeded $20,000 for three hours. Wow. Not to mention the charges are listed in code and acronyms so the consumer is unable to identify each charge, even if they wanted to.

REV CODE	HCPCS	BILLING DESCRIPTION	QTY	AMOUNT	CHARGE NUMBER	SERVICE DATE
0250	A4216	NACL10ML PFS IJ	1	8.98	005324200	12/02/2016
0255	Q9967	LOCM 1ML	100	2,113.00	005356209	12/02/2016
0250	J7030	NACL .9 1L IVF	1	431.79	005412670	12/02/2016
0300	80048	BSC METABLC PNL	1	614.32	004100166	12/02/2016
0300	81001	UA AUTO W/MICRO	1	167.53	004101001	12/02/2016
0300	85025	CBC/DIFF&PLATLT	1	305.55	004105028	12/02/2016
0300	87086	CULT URIN CNT	1	554.54	004107086	12/02/2016
0350	74177	CT AB/PEL W/CM	1	9,409.00	005054177	12/02/2016
0402	76970	US SCROTUM	1	1,143.59	005066782	12/02/2016
0450	96361	IV HYD ADD HR	1	174.60	006100761	12/02/2016
0450	96374	INJ T/P/D IVP	1	432.22	006100774	12/02/2016
0450	96375	INJ ADD SEQ IVP	2	864.44	006100775	12/02/2016
0450	99284	ER VISIT LVL IV	1	2,818.12	006100526	12/01/2016
0636	J1170	HYDROMORP4MG IJ	1	80.76	005327592	12/02/2016
0636	J1885	KETOROLAC 15MG	2	247.98	005321633	12/02/2016
0636	J2405	ONDANSETRO1MGIJ	4	321.60	005322936	12/02/2016

TOTAL   19,908.02

Understanding Your Statement...

A The services you received during your stay at the Hospital

B Total dollar amount charged by the Hospital for services delivered

C Total statement charges on your account

D The dollar amount reduced due to an insurance contractual adjustment or other discount

E The amount paid by one or more insurance companies to the Hospital on behalf of the patient

F The amount already paid to the Hospital by the patient or their guarantor

G The amount due from the patient as indicated on the provider bill or statement

A		B
Dates of Activity	**Item Description / Activity**	**Charges**
12/02/2016 - 12/02/2016	LABORATORY SERVICES	$1,861.94
12/02/2016 - 12/02/2016	DIAGNOSTIC/THERAPEUTIC IMAGING	$10,552.59
12/02/2016 - 12/02/2016	PHARMACY	$3,204.11
12/01/2016 - 12/02/2016	EMERGENCY ROOM	$4,289.38

Nonprofit credit counseling services may be available in the area. State and federal law requires debt collectors to treat you fairly, and prohibit debt collectors from using profane language or making improper communications with third parties, including your employer.

If you have insurance coverage, Medicare, Medi-Cal, or other coverage for this date of service, as a courtesy, we may file a claim for you. Please contact us to provide insurance information by calling customer service at the number indicated below or return a copy of the front and back of your insurance card along with the payment slip in the envelope provided. If you do not have insurance for this date of service, the account balance listed above is your responsibility. However, if you do not have health insurance coverage, you may be eligible for coverage through the California Health Benefit Exchange, Medicare, Medi-Cal, California Children's Services Program, other state or county funded programs or charity care. You may obtain a Medi-Cal application online at http://www.dhcs.ca.gov/services/medi-cal/Pages/ApplyforMedi-Cal.aspx. You may obtain a California Health Benefit Exchange application online at: http://www.coveredca.com/. Other governmental program information is available upon request from the telephone number below.

If you lack, or have inadequate, insurance, and meet certain low- and moderate-income

C	**Total Charges**	$19,908.02
D	**Account Adjustments**	$8,421.09
E	**Paid by Insurance**	$7,970.85
F	**Paid by Patient**	$0.00
G	**Remaining Balance**	$3,516.08

Thank you for choosing   Amount you owe now $3,516.08

After adjustments and all the other financing games hospitals play, my responsibility was only a combined $4,500. For three hours and a few tests. So they could tell me my boy was fine.

While I was grateful he was fine, I called the hospital to discuss the bill and request a discount. The operator advised that they were unwilling to negotiate. I did not send payment and waited four months until collectors started to call. Most hospital companies own their own collection agency, and they refer outstanding invoices over for more aggressive collection tactics from what patients perceive to be an "independent" collection agency. Despite the name, the collection agency is owned by the hospital. The hospital-owned collection agency will then try for a few months to collect before turning the invoice over to an independent collection agency after four more months. The hospital sells each invoice for ten cents on the dollar to a true collection agency, who then pursues the patient even more aggressively.

While the internal agency would not negotiate with me, in most cases the external agency will. The entire business model is to recover their expense plus additional margin. I sought justice as a result of a calculated decision by the hospital to avoid transparent pricing. Pricing transparency is an issue that must be addressed by employers when shopping for their insurance company. Very few hospitals provide patients with prices in advance of procedures, and most do not make them readily accessible to patients even when requested.

Whether Obamacare or an entirely new model, value-based care is here to stay. There is no alternative for the federal government as the Medicare fund is still on track to be empty in the near future (recent projections show it being empty by 2029) due to the volume of baby boomers retiring daily. And as for the private market, insurers have been all-in with value-based care, or managed care, for years, as it's an effective and lucrative business model. FFS and managed care are on two opposite ends of the spectrum. One was a free-for-all, and the other has tight restrictions that must be met before rendering care. No wonder hospitals and doctors continue to resist transitioning to managed care. Managed care came with rules and oversight, two things they were unaccustomed to and did not want to deal with.

After President Obama made healthcare reform his top priority, his goals included making access to healthcare available to all Americans and, at the same time, attempting to restructure the financial model to address the rapidly depleting Medicare fund. The only path to controlling healthcare spending was a conversion to a managed care model. For Medicare patients, there was already a proven model that had emerged in recent years: Medicare Advantage. In Medicare Advantage, seniors consent to a managed care provider managing their Medicare benefit in exchange for some added benefits. The Medicare Advantage model has proven to be more financially viable for the government, which simply issues a flat amount of money to the insurer on behalf of each patient each month. The insurer is in turn responsible for any care needed (often referred to as *full-risk*). Medicare Advantage is a form of managed care for American seniors who qualify for Medicare benefits, and it includes checks and balances in the form of preauthorization.

Obamacare was also designed in large part to end the heads-in-beds mentality. Essentially, almost every care coordination incentive and penalty in Obamacare was implemented to prevent unnecessary hospitalization and institutionalization. In short, the federal government was telling providers, "If you admit someone to a hospital or nursing home who did not need to be there and could have been cared for at a lower level of care, we are not going to pay you, and we are also going to fine you."

It's a simple reality to legislators: there will be no money left in the Medicare fund in the near future, and reverting to a model that allows doctors and providers to bill for services at-will is no longer an option.

As a result, America is rapidly becoming a completely managed care environment for healthcare. This should theoretically rein in healthcare spending—but don't count on it. Free spending and aggressive lobbying by insurers and hospitals are the norm in healthcare, so this conversion will take time. However, the ultimate goal of the new managed care models is to control spending.

Almost every payer (health plan or insurance company) that has traditionally reimbursed physicians based on how many patients they see each day has now converted to alternative reimbursement methodologies that represent some form of managed care. They started this transition shortly after Obamacare was passed, and for many, it is already complete. For Medicare, however, the aggressive push is taking a lot longer. Doctors and hospitals are dragging their feet every chance they get, as the new model is a threat to their ability to drive volume and resulting income.

However, in time, with the exception of a few lagging and aging physicians who are set in their FFS ways and have yet to retire, behaviors will change, and an entirely new mind-set for physicians and health systems will be in place in coming years. The trend toward managed Medicare will continue.

One of the primary goals of Obamacare was to initiate a national transformation to a patient-centered delivery model. In a patient-centered model, the first question that should be asked by doctors when patients are hospitalized should simply be this: "Can this patient be cared for at home, and if so, what resources are needed to ensure a safe discharge?" This philosophy is at the heart of the "hospital at home" methodology. The goal of "hospital at home" is simply to utilize self-management, technology, and resources to treat and care for ailments at home rather than the traditionally required institutionalization.

The biggest challenge during the FFS era, as alluded to in the story of my grandmother, was that no one ever educated her or the family that she had a choice in where to go after her hospital stay. They also never asked her if she wanted to go to a nursing home at all, or if she preferred to go home.

As a business executive, remember this when your employee goes to the hospital: That employee has a choice every step of the way. Empower them to question the doctor when something is not completely clear.

If you take away just a few nuggets from this book, let one of them be this: This is America, and as patients, whether in the FFS era or post-Obamacare, you ultimately have a choice of your provider and what type of care you will be given.

But even with value-based care (managed care, as it is more commonly known) now entrenched in American healthcare, the biggest flaw in the delivery system remains: Anyone on American soil can access healthcare services in any emergency room in the country, at any time.

Yep, that's a fact. To clarify, the hospital or doctor is not legally allowed to ask the patient or family any questions about money or insurance until after the care has been provided. It's the law.

Let me explain. In 1986, the Emergency Medical Treatment and Active Labor Act (EMTALA) was passed, requiring hospitals to provide necessary medical care to any patient who showed up in their emergency room in active labor or with an emergent need. Hospitals are required by law to provide needed care without ever asking if the patient is able to pay until after care is ordered or delivered.

EMTALA, in a sense, guarantees free access to care for anyone in America, including foreigners, in any emergency room nationwide. Even though the law is specific to individuals in active labor or with an emergent need, the hospital must see the patient to assess if the need is emergent before they can deny them access. Thus, every individual is guaranteed an emergency room consult, whether they are insured or not, for any reason at all. The hospital's liability is significant if they were to turn any patient away without a consult. As a result, most uninsured or low-income families with minimal health benefits often simply use the emergency department whenever needed and do not even have a personal family doctor. As you are likely aware, the cost of operating an emergency department is significant—much higher than the cost of operating a doctor's office—so this trend puts a significant financial strain on the system and contributes to America's affordability crisis. It also results in added financial strain on hospitals in inner-city areas. In summary, the highest cost level of delivery—the emergency room—is the only level of care utilized by many uninsured Americans.

The American tax payer, your business and your family, are ultimately footing the bill for this.

As a result of EMTALA and hospitals being required to consult everyone who shows up to the emergency room, it is important for the reader to understand two key principles about care delivery in the emergency room, specifically:

- Prior to examining a patient and providing emergency care, hospitals and doctors are not permitted legally to ask if the patient has insurance or who their insurance provider is.

- Hospitals and doctors must approach all patients in the emergency room in the same manner, as they are unaware if the patient is covered by managed care or not.

As a result of these regulations, hospitals were forced to capture additional revenue from paying patients who were insured, and overutilization (ordering several often-unnecessary labs or tests) of patients became the norm during the FFS era. This was a result of several factors:

- Liability. Doctors would rather be safe than sorry. And hey, why not, we all get paid more if we order more tests!

- Relationships, nepotism, or quid pro quo. Call it what you want, but doctors adhere to the principle of "you scratch my back (financially), and I will scratch yours in return." The more tests that were ordered, the more doctors got involved and billed.

- Justification. Let us not forget the almighty quest for justification, in any way, shape, or form, to admit an emergency department patient to the hospital. We must go fishing for at least some medical reason to back it up! Heads in beds, whatever it takes.

Fast forward through forty years of creating and implementing these habits, and in 2011, when managed care was mandated by Obamacare, the payer world began to be turned upside down. There were no more widgets to bill for, no more heads-in-beds reimbursement, no more reward for volume. It's a managed care world now. And all patients, seniors in particular, must be treated as managed care, whether they are or not.

Making this problem even worse is the fact that this generation of Americans rarely has a long-term personal physician. Remember the days of having a personal family physician? You could call him or her in the middle of the night and walk into their office anytime without an appointment, and they would meet you at the hospital when you were injured or ill. That's no longer the case. The reason? Look no further than managed care.

As discussed, the term "managed care" emerged in the 1980s as a means to control of laissez-faire behavior of doctors and providers by requiring the insurer to preauthorize any services ordered by a doctor or hospital. Managed care is intended to be a service-driven model, and "features" include limited access for patients, restrictions, required preauthorization, and a constant messaging to live a healthy lifestyle.

In regard to managed care contracting, your primary care physician may not contract with any of the insurance plans offered through your business's contracted provider. Americans change jobs often; the likelihood of an individual taking a new job with a company whose contracted insurance provider does not contract with his or her desired primary care physician is high. And if your insurance provider is an HMO, it's even more likely that your doctor will not contract with your insurer.

There are several reasons this may affect your personal physician. The hospital may no longer allow your primary care physician to see patients in the hospital. Or, just as likely, your doctor may have chosen to no longer see patients in the hospital for financial reasons. For example, the reimbursement for consulting one patient in the hospital each day may not justify the time it takes the doctor to leave his or her office, drive to the hospital, visit with the patient, document the necessary treatment, and drive back to the office. Financially, the doctor is better off in most cases just remaining in the offices and attempting to consult one patient every ten minutes for six hours of the day to earn his or her desired income.

The age of physician specialization is upon us. Many family doctors and primary care physicians are no longer credentialed to even care for patients in a hospital setting, let alone a post-acute setting. The financial structure and incentives of the FFS era led doctors to choose their preferred business model. Very few still have an active office practice and care for patients in the hospital. In fact, the few doctors who maintain an active office practice and also see patients in hospitals and post-acute facilities almost all have hired partners, nurse practitioners (NPs), or physicians assistants to support them in adequately fulfilling all these obligations.

So while you may still have a personal family physician, it is likely that your physician would not care for you should you be admitted to the hospital. So who cares for you in the hospital? A hospitalist.

To explain the motivation for hospitals converting to hospitalist models, we must reflect back on hospital financial incentives. Medicare reimbursed hospitals on an episode-based methodology during the FFS era. This meant that regardless of how long the patient remained in the hospital, the hospital was being paid a flat rate or lump sum, depending on the patient's diagnosis, severity, and comorbidities. Reimbursement was not at all tied to how long the patient remained in the hospital. Thus, hospitals quickly realized that the shorter length of time that a patient was in the hospital, the more profitable that patient's care would be for the hospital. Managing a patient's "length of stay" became a top priority. Many primary care physicians, who in the 1990s were still caring for their patients when they were hospitalized, had a tough time meeting hospitals' demand to shorten length of stay.

The hospital's financial incentive is to shorten the length of stay to maximize reimbursement, in contradiction to the physician's incentive to lengthen the length of stay for a few extra days of reimbursement. As a result, the hospital decided to employ or organize doctors into hospitalists groups and compensate them to ensure they were focused on the hospitals financial incentives.

For example, hospital nursing teams conduct rounds each morning with an assigned medical director (doctor) to review each patient in the hospital. If, during morning rounds, the care team determines that a patient is ready to be discharged or will be ready by the day's end, the attending physician is notified, as he or she is required to write a discharge order in the chart before the patient is eligible for discharge. For private-practice doctors, if the hospital calls at 10 a.m. to advise a patient is ready and needs a discharge order written, the doctor may not be able to get to the hospital until that night to write the order. This is known as a discharge delay. In some cases, the doctor was not planning to visit the hospital at all that day and would wait until the next morning.

Hospitals quickly realized that they could not rely on these private-practice physicians to reply and write discharge orders in a timely manner. Thus, hospitals began contracting for "hospitalist" services. A hospitalist is a doctor who is contracted with the hospital for the sole purpose of managing patients in that hospital. Their top priority each day is to identify patients who are ready for discharge and make sure those patients are discharged in a timely manner.

Over time, use of hospitalists became more and more common, to the point that many hospitals converted to an entirely hospitalist model and no longer permitted private-practice physicians to consult patients within the hospital. The hospitalist model is even more prevalent and necessary in managed care than it was in the

FFS era, so it is likely to continue being the norm in a post-PPACA environment. In fact, most managed care organizations do not use the hospital's hospitalist group but contract with their own group of hospitalists to ensure that the doctors' incentives are aligned with the managed care organization and not the hospital.

It is ironic when you think about it. Hospitals contracted with hospitalist groups in the FFS era for two very specific reasons:

- First and foremost, they were to admit as many patients as possible to drive as much inpatient revenue as possible to the hospital.

- Then, once a patient is admitted to the hospital, hospitalists were to immediately start planning and developing a care plan to discharge the patient as soon as possible to maximize the reimbursement.

That's it. "Get 'em in and then get 'em out!" That was the secret to running a hospital in the FFS era, and the team of hospitalists in each hospital was responsible for fulfilling this mission.

To take that point even further, physician specialization has evolved; post-acute care doctors have employed a hospitalist model as well, to once again ensure that the hospital's financial incentives are the priority. Coincidentally the SNF's financial incentive is to extend length of stay, in contradiction to the hospitals desire to shorten it. These contracted post-acute specialists are referred to as "SNFists." In most cases, these contracted SNFists do not have a private practice and do not care for patients in hospitals. They simply spend their entire day consulting patients in SNFs and other post-acute facilities.

Remember in Chapter 2, when we talked about hospitals having a competitive bidding process for physician services within the hospital, where the winner was whoever could prove they would put the most heads in beds? Hospitalists are actually guiltier of this than any others, including emergency physicians. When the emergency doctor wants to admit a patient to the hospital, he or she must first contact the hospitalist to write the hospital admission order. Capitalism rears its ugly head once again as when patients are in the gray area of needing to be admitted, they often are admitted simply as a result of the process. To explain, the emergency department doctor picking up the phone or texting a hospitalist to order the consult was itself all the justification needed for a hospitalist to write an admission order in the FFS era—good formula if you are a hospital CEO!

From a capitalistic perspective, you could summarize the move to the hospitalist model by simply stating that the hospital had to buy the loyalty of the doctor in order to align financial incentives—and not just the emergency room doctors but the attending doctors as well. And that led to the emergence of hospitalists. In a way, it's a "you're either with us or against us" approach to ensure that doctors' incentives are aligned with the hospital's. To explain, a personal family physician was likely to be more receptive and loyal to the requests of the hospitalized patient or their family. A doctor employed by the hospital was very clear on the incentive to admit as many patients as possible and then discharge them as quickly as possible to maximize reimbursement. The patient and family had no prior relationship with the hospitalist, so their input was not a priority: the bottom line was. This is why the days of a personal family physician have gone by the wayside.

The reality is that even in what we refer to as traditional Medicare FFS, there are so many new penalty and incentive programs for doctors, hospitals, and other providers that even the traditional FFS product is significantly value-based. These penalties focus on quality factors, criteria-based decision making, infection rates, avoidable readmission rates, and referral patterns for post-acute care, among other topics.

So how does this affect you? What about your business or employer? Well for one, it is capitalism, and change brings added expense. While access expanded as a result of Obamacare, costs skyrocketed for many. It was a prime example of the redistribution of wealth in America. In fact, in many cases family health costs reached a Health-Wealth tipping point that led families to opt out of health insurance altogether—myself included for a short time, as discussed previously.

Many providers and physicians are still struggling to see how they will fit in a managed care model, which is completely understandable. This transition is done in the name of more effective, patient-centered care. The federal government loosely describes *patient-centered care* as an approach that focuses more on the patient and less on how physicians and providers are reimbursed. Another common cliché is "from volume to value." That simply means we are making a shift from a volume-based reimbursement methodology to a value-based methodology that rewards physicians and providers for reducing utilization (testing, appointments, and so on).

Because this change is a threat to the income of both doctors and providers, there has been significant reluctance to convert to a managed care model from both doctors and providers. This reluctance by doctors and hospitals to convert, as it threatened their revenue model, is why many of the Obamacare policies were put in place — to force this behavior to change. It became a mandate to convert, but providers and doctors were given several years to make the conversion. Most providers and doctors did little to start the conversion to managed care until just months before the PPACA deadlines began in 2014, as the hospital lobby, as well as the American Medical

Association (AMA) physician lobby, is one of the most historically influential lobbies in the country. In short, doctors and hospitals refused to move, hoped for a change of heart through lobbying, and when it did not happen, they scrambled to implement plans to meet minimum requirements dictated by Obamacare in the final months before the deadline. Managed care is a threat to their income; there is no way around it. Welcome to the real world. It's a world of accountability and required criteria.

Even with Obamacare giving way to GOP tweaks during the Trump administration, the Obama era made access to healthcare a much higher priority in American society as a whole. It is important to note that an entire generation, the millennials, have now been raised during their impressionable years in an era in which healthcare for the first time became a right to all Americans. Society has now become conditioned and accepting to this issue and equally as important, the topic has now been prioritized for more than seven years. Just like in business, you cannot giveth and then taketh away. Whether it's a pay raise or added benefit, the American way has always been that once something is given, it can't be taken back. With this in mind, it is important to note that regardless of political affiliation, American public opinion in regard to the access to healthcare has shifted dramatically since 2010. Again, I am not referring to the politically charged debate of how healthcare benefits for low-income patients are paid for but simply stating that it's not just millennials who view access to healthcare as a right to every American; many Americans have been conditioned to this belief after living with the reality for seven years.

So if healthcare is a right to all Americans, and we have freedom of choice to go to whichever doctor or hospital we choose, why won't hospitals disclose their prices for each procedure? Great question.

They have never been formally asked or required to disclose prices. And because healthcare costs are negotiated on an individual's behalf by a third party, there has never been great demand for transparency in pricing. That trend must end. Employers and insurers must insist that hospitals be more transparent.

To make the problem worse, doctors were ordering a significant volume of unnecessary tests and getting paid by the federal government and insurers even when the tests are unjustified. Significant amounts of money were being wasted annually on excessive testing and treatment.

Hospitals are not the only entity lacking transparency in pricing. Pharmaceutical companies, doctors, and device manufacturers are just as guilty. Let me share one example of wasteful spending in the name of capitalism.

It was a Friday afternoon in 2006, and I was concerned; our revenue collection projection illustrated that we would likely not have the necessary $240,000 required to be in the bank the following Tuesday to cover payroll. We were probably going to be $20,000 short, and we had no reserves. There had been at least three pay periods in the prior year where I had to ask my chief financial officer and chief nursing officer to join me in holding our paychecks for a few days to ensure that we did not bounce checks. Our company did not allow auto-deposit of employee paychecks, simply as a cash flow management tactic, so no employees had paychecks auto-deposited, even as late as 2006.

One of the primary challenges for me as hospital CEO was that my hospital was a safety net hospital, designated by the government to serve the neediest of the needy. We served a disproportionate share of unfunded patients in comparison to other hospitals in the region. We rarely had any cash reserves and basically lived day-today, stashing as much revenue as we could to ensure we could cover payroll every two weeks.

After two years on the job, I was starting to get familiar with tendencies and habits of the active doctors at my hospital. So after eating lunch with doctors in the physician dining room that Friday afternoon and returning to my office, I recalled that two days prior, one of my cardiologists, Dr. Jones (a pseudonym, to ensure privacy), had called to ask if there were any days he could pick up on the hospitalist panel (if any doctors were seeking to get covered for a day or two due to vacations, etc.), as he was having a low volume (of patients) month at the office and in the hospital and was hoping to still hit his monthly financial projection. He had reached out to me with the same request at least four times in the prior two years.

While he knew that there were rarely cancellations on the call panel and that most doctors just swapped shifts without involving me, I advised him that I would make a few calls on his behalf to see if anyone was interested in giving up a shift. To explain, the call panel assigned patients who showed up in the emergency department to a specific assigned doctor (unless the patient specifically requested a personal physician who was credentialed at our hospital and available).

In addition to making a few calls on his behalf, I had picked up on a few trends in prior months that would routinely occur in the days following his calls requesting to pick up a shift.

- First, I would see an increase in referrals to him for cardiology consults from primary care doctors in the hospital. This led to the question of necessity, as these patients rarely had needs justifying these referrals and there were no checks and balances in place to confirm.

- Second, I would see the late addition (on Thursday afternoon) of multiple cardiology procedures for Dr. Jones's patients added to the hospital schedule for his Friday procedures.

- Third, on Friday afternoons, when the procedures were complete and the results were reviewed by Dr. Jones, at least one of the three to five patients he tested that day would need a pacemaker installed.

The result of each of these three trends was increased procedures with no checks or balances to confirm necessity. Each also resulted in increased revenue for Dr. Jones.

The third trend listed was the killer, as a pacemaker was a hard cost to the hospital of approximately $9,000. Dr. Jones was notorious for providing services to unfunded (meaning they had no insurance) or low-reimbursing Medicaid patients. He could have cared less that the hospital took a loss of at least $10,000 for this patient, considering the testing time and costs, operating room time for installation, staff wages, and hard cost of $9,000. Because he still got paid by Medicaid, it was the hospital that took the loss.

Medicaid is the name for the government healthcare welfare program. This patient was a Medicaid patient, and Medicaid did not reimburse hospitals any money for pacemakers; they are an "included service" in the $1,100 a day Medicaid paid hospitals. Pacemaker patients often only stayed one or two days; our cost per day for inpatient care averaged about $1,500, so the loss was in excess of $10,000 to the hospital whether the patient had Medicaid or no payer source at all.

On this particular Friday, Dr. Jones called me just after lunch to advise me that he needed a pacemaker for a procedure that afternoon.

I explained we did not have the cash on hand, and I asked him if a pacemaker was the only or best solution and if any alternative approaches could be considered. Dr. Jones was notorious for being a yeller, and as expected, he yelled into the phone that the procedure started in two hours and if the pacemaker and device sales representative were not present on time, he would turn the hospital in (report us) to regulators for failing to provide adequate resources to ensure appropriate patient care.

So I hung up the phone and called the pacemaker device vendor. For this procedure, the sales representative would routinely assist the physician in the operating room during the procedure to ensure proper installation. The sales representative told me that he had been advised by his boss that he could not deliver any more product to my hospital until at least one of the two outstanding invoices we had was paid, as they were both more than 120 days delinquent. The reason I was calling this device company was because the only other manufacturer that supplied us had refused to work with us and notified us of pending legal action a week prior for our past-due balance in excess of $80,000 for devices they had supplied. I had no other options.

I made an emotional appeal to the vendor simply asking for his understanding, and it worked. Thirty minutes after I had informed Dr. Jones that the device would be delivered on time, the unthinkable happened. Dr. Jones called back and advised me that he needed another pacemaker for a separate patient. Both procedures were scheduled for later that same afternoon. And both were Medicaid patients.

I called the device representative back. He answered and told me that he was en route to the hospital. When his boss got on the phone, I advised him of the situation and made a startling request. "I am requesting that each of you forego your sales commission for each of these two devices, request a manufacturer discount on at least one, and as a result offer me both devices for the price of one." I added that the hospital was essentially eating the cost on both, as they were both for patients with no insurance or ability to pay, and that I was seeking goodwill to accommodate these patients in need.

The silence that followed was deafening. I had played the underinsured card hard and added that they should have to assume some of the burden as well. I stated that I was aware that the sales distributor's commission on each sale was at least $3,000, and if they would waive it on these two, it would make up almost the entire discount I was looking for.

So each of the three parties (the hospital, the vendor and the supplier) involved in supplying the plastic pacemaker to my hospital was collecting $3,000 for what was essentially a plastic device likely costing only $20 to manufacture, and I was expected to write a check for $9,000 each time one was needed. They initially seemed appalled that I would make such claims and even make such a request, as I represented the hospital, and it was my responsibility.

That was the problem. The hospital was responsible for the patient as a result of EMTALA and we were forbidden from denying service.

This chapter illustrates that regardless of the delivery model, so long as healthcare is free in the emergency department as a result of EMTALA, American businesses and taxpayers will continue to be faced with increased premiums each year to offset those costs. While the FFS free-for-all—where there was no accountability for doctors and hospitals—gives way to managed care, that is likely to slow cost increases, but not significantly enough to prevent annual premium increases being handed to American businesses. As a young hospital CEO still learning the ropes of the business, when I returned to work

Monday after the eventful Friday afternoon in which we found a way to get a vendor to deliver two pacemakers, I returned with a different outlook on the industry.

Although it was probably one of the worst ways to start the work week, I approached the six highest-paid employees at my hospital and asked them if they would be willing to hold their paychecks for a few days (along with me) after payday that next Friday. It was one of the most demoralizing and embarrassing requests I ever had to make to this day as an executive, but I made it happen. And I made sure the vendor was paid off fully within two weeks, as agreed to. And we were also able to cover payrolls that week with the funds in our account…barely!

As long as there is free care in the emergency department, American businesses, as well as upper and middle-class American taxpayers will continue to pay for the free medical care provided to the uninsured and underinsured. PPACA could not solve the affordability crisis, nor will any GOP plan, so long as care remains accessible and free in American emergency rooms. Offsetting healthcare costs in America has been one of the largest redistributions of wealth in our country's history. Your business and your family are being burdened with this responsibility. Yet no one is holding the hospital industry or insurers accountable for its outdated and irresponsible practices that have resulted in an affordability crisis in America.

As the financial steward of your company's healthcare delivery partners, when will you say enough is enough? Has your company reached its Health-Wealth tipping point? Realize in this moment that the tipping point has likely passed, but your organization is counting on you, and you can mark the occasion today by making a change and choosing Health-Wealth. Don't let healthcare bankrupt your business like it has so many others in America. The change starts here.

CHAPTER 4

MILLENNIAL CULTURE MEETS HEALTHCARE: KEEPING PATIENTS HEALTHY AND AT HOME

I WALKED INTO 24 Hour Fitness a few months back for my not-so-regular weekly workout and entered my phone number on a keyboard and then scanned my fingerprint to confirm it was me. Ten seconds later I walked into the gym. Wow, that was simple—modern technology. This process makes me feel like a hip millennial!

But why can't hospitals simplify in this manner?

What if each time someone walked into an emergency room anywhere in America, we had at our fingertips a complete medical record since birth for that patient? What if alongside the EMR, there was cloud-based software that also allowed input from providers, family members, and caretakers of our conversations, observations, and other things pertaining to the social determinants of healthcare, which are often more relevant than the EMR history itself?

What if it simply took a fingerprint and an identification number to access this complete personal history? Either way, it would move us closer to personalized medicine, instant registration and reduced wait times for patients, and decreased nonproductive time for physicians and hospitals. This is my vision for the future of healthcare. If 24 Hour Fitness can do it, why can't billion-dollar healthcare systems?

With that in mind, other questions arise. Why don't we already have more data about patients? Why don't we know more about patients when they show up in the emergency department? Why is it so difficult for health systems to get connected electronically to know more about their patients? With all the software providers and innovations available, shouldn't we be further along in terms of knowing more about an individual's health history than we do at present?

These are all valid questions. I get asked these questions a lot. The answer is simple: Hospitals have had this technology available to them for years but have chosen not to purchase or implement it. After all, it was not conducive to their "don't ask, don't tell, just admit, then bill" approach to caring for patients in the emergency department.

In the FFS era, the fact is that hospital operators did not want to know more about patients who were showing up to the emergency department. After all, if hospitals had information to prove a patient was not in fact ill or injured, then the hospital would not have been able to admit them to the inpatient floor of the hospital and bill for the care delivered. Remember, heads in beds was the name of the game. Why would the hospital want to know anything more about a patient than it had to know?

Think about it this way. Hospitals have always been paid for putting heads in beds. Oftentimes, a patient shows up to the hospital, and the hospital acts like they know absolutely nothing about the patient. What a great way to justify admitting the patient so that the hospital and physician could get paid for ordering tests and putting a head in a bed. This scenario often happens even when the very same patient came to the hospital emergency department the day prior and had been sent home.

That's it. That is where our desire for more knowledge ends. This may seem laughable, but this is an accurate example of how our country has operated for the last thirty years. The hospital has always been the power player—the king of the hill. The hospital has been the most influential player in the continuum and had the checkbook to make the decisions. So in a model where the hospital is paid for putting heads in beds, why would the hospital invest in technology that could hinder its ability to admit patients? During the FFS era, there was little incentive for the hospital to invest in advanced technology and EMRs.

The federal government put an end to that myopic mentality when they passed Obamacare, which included aggressive mandates for hospitals to implement EMR systems. These mandates are referred to as "meaningful use" and were implemented in phases. Hospitals were penalized if they did not adhere to these deadlines. The passing of Obamacare and the implementation of a value-based delivery model put tremendous pressure on health systems to do the right thing for the patient in a myriad of ways.

So in short, you have these gigantic software providers and EMR companies, and they send an army of sales and tech-support people into the hospital. Essentially, these juggernaut EMR providers have not accomplished even the simplest of tasks that would be in the best interest of the patient. While many health systems are getting closer to the model described above, the fact of the matter that I observed, is that the technology has been there for several years, even predating Obamacare, in many cases. However, it simply was not in the best interests of the hospitals to create that model. The reality is, hospitals still only get paid for putting heads in beds, but all the incentives and penalties in Obamacare were designed to make sure that only the right heads are put into beds. Thus, if hospitals still employ a philosophy of "find a way to justify admitting every patient we can from the emergency room," they will be penalized excessively. As a result, the limit access to information and admit at all cost model is not a viable model moving forward.

In 2016, as I consulted hospital CEOs across the country, several prominent executives confided in me that their most significant operational challenge in transforming to value-based care was getting the support of their own hospital-based doctors and case management staff. And even those executives who felt they had the full support of their case managers were expressing frustration that the journey to taking a "discharge home first" mentality within their hospital was proving to be difficult, if not impossible.

As discussed earlier, the incentives of the FFS free-for-all led to deep-rooted cultural practices and behaviors among doctors. The pattern became to discharge patients to institutions such as nursing homes or acute rehab facilities after a hospital stay. Not only did it reduce the liability of the doctor and hospital (should the patient return home and then have a fall or unfortunate incident after they were discharged), but it also became the easiest and quickest way to discharge a patient from the hospital as you did not have to coordinate a pickup with the family or, potentially, for additional resources (equipment or drugs) needed at home. Yes! The path of least resistance became the preference for all involved. So instead of going home after a hospital stay, seniors were routinely discharged from the acute hospital to nursing homes, whether it was necessary or not.

As time went on—three decades in all—doctors got much better at justifying why nursing homes were supposedly a "better and safer" option for patients upon discharge than "taking the risk of going home." Their communication and scripting for families and patients got smoother and smoother until they had it down. It became the accepted norm that institutionalizing patients on discharge from the hospital was the more appropriate path for discharging.

So patients and their families were led to feel that, by returning home, they would be unsafe and potentially at risk … in their own home. That's not just manipulative but also extremely powerful when you look at it from a distance, isn't it: convincing every patient that they are unsafe and at risk in their own home without considering each patient's unique circumstances, home environment and support system. It seems pretty cavalier on the surface as well. I always jokingly ask when I say, "Raise your hand if you can't wait for the day that you personally get to be admitted to a nursing home for the rest of your life!"

Combine that with long-standing Medicare regulations that ensure Americans have a choice in choosing a post-acute facility, and doctors felt empowered to control the process. All the doctor had to do was get the patient to agree with his or her recommendation, and the path of least resistance became the norm. That's right, seniors with Medicare were discharged to a nursing home in most cases, unless they were educated enough on the laws to challenge the discharge order, the doctor, or the case manager and the system as a whole.

Here is the point: hospitals and physicians are driving up your costs and unnecessarily spending your company dollars even after the patient leaves the hospital. In addition to driving up costs for businesses and families, these unjustified, long-standing habits contradict individual patient preferences.

Without personal ownership of decision making and cost comparison in healthcare, there will be little change. The common terminology used to describe this issue in the healthcare field is *self-management*. Without self-management and accountability, there will be no momentum or support to drive change in America's healthcare delivery system. Patients and families must learn that they cannot trust the opinion of just one doctor, hospital employee, or insurance representative; they must learn to ask questions and do research on their own to ensure optimal health and pricing transparency. Without self-management or a caretaker that makes the commitment to learn, decreased community health and lower cost efficiencies in care delivery will continue to plague the industry.

America's healthcare affordability crisis is worse than ever, and without personal accountability and education on health and wellness, the crisis will only get worse. So self-management and wellness are no longer simply luxuries for the wealthy; they are synonymous with living a healthier lifestyle. Remember just a few years ago when the word "wellness" came with connotations of Eastern medicine and a physician office lobby with calming water fountains, harmonious instrumentals, and an aroma reminiscent of a fully bloomed flower garden? Not anymore. Wellness and healthy lifestyles are two of the most common traits of our youngest generations.

Many employers have invested in workplace fitness and health incentive programs for employees. These programs offer rewards, similar to credit card points or frequent flier miles, for making healthy decisions such as quitting smoking, increasing exercise or steps daily, reducing body fat ratio, and eating healthier foods. It's important to note that these programs don't necessarily just reward that fitness fanatic who sits in the office next to you at work and carries her own water bottle with her each day (often with some odd-colored concoction that we are told is some type of unique formula that burns body fat mysteriously). These programs reward everyone who shows improvement and it is often the individual that began the program with the worst habits and shows improvement that can benefit the most in the long run—both in life and in rewards points!

Similar to employers emphasizing health and wellness, some universities are taking the same approach by requiring students to wear Fitbits and translating their physical activity into a fitness grade. What a great example of how technology is opening doors for millennials that no other generation has had the luxury of benefitting from in their teen and college years. Another example of this transition to healthy lifestyles is the gyms that are popping up nationwide, catering to the middle-aged and the baby boomer generation. These gyms are often outpatient rehabilitation facilities that also serve as long-term workout facilities for aging adults. Although the insurer often pays for the first few weeks of recovery and rehab in these facilities, the gyms were created so that individuals can pay privately to continue coming even when they are back to full health (a "twenty-four-hour fitness" for seniors). One example of this is in Southern California. Dr. Sheldon Zinberg, founder of Caremore, created the concept of Nifty-After-Fifty, a gym designed specifically for seniors. The concept has been so successful that other medical groups and insurers have joined together to invest in these facilities.

These gyms have equipment not only for physician health but also have computers that test and stimulate mental and cognitive growth. Many of these facilities also have dietitians, occupational therapists, nurses, physical therapists, and other skilled healthcare workers on-site for a few hours every week to provide access and support to members.

It's a genius idea when you think about it. The medical insurer, who is financially responsible for your health, is creating an environment that you pay for privately and separately to improve your health. It becomes a desired social routine for many, as well as an integral part of their lifestyle. It's a senior center for active seniors—just don't tell the individuals working out there that they are seniors!

On that note, one thing you will learn working in healthcare is that no one thinks they are old or sick. If you have not yet learned that from your grandfather or grandmother, you learn it quickly when you work in the senior healthcare space. No one thinks they are old. It is human nature. Do you know how many years my grandmother could be heard saying, "I am the youngest person living in this retirement community. The rest of them are old"? She said that right up until her death in her mid-eighties (bless her heart!). But let's do the math here. It's a senior community that required all residents be sixty or older, and she lived there for twenty years. So while it may have been true that she was one of the younger folks when she moved in, it turns out I was the typical gullible grandchild who, twenty years later, was still believing her when she would take me to the shuffleboard park and tell me she was the youngest resident in the park. Looking back, there was a fat chance of that being true in her eighties!

All this considered, it is likely that insurers will start providing financial incentives to patients who live healthier lifestyles. It is likely that regulations will begin allowing insurers more liberty in returning cash discounts to patients who commit to healthy lifestyles and consent to electronic monitoring to prove it. Sound familiar? It's the same approach that auto insurers have been taking to discount auto rates for years. Healthcare insurers are slower to change, as healthcare is one of the most highly regulated industries in the world, and healthcare finance is no exception to those stringent regulations.

Qualcomm and UnitedHealth announced a program in early 2016 called United Healthcare Motion that gives enrollees in United Healthcare insurance plans wearable devices that have the ability to track how many steps they take each day. Employees who use the devices can earn up to $1,460 per year in savings, which will be placed in a health savings account (HSA). The transformation to healthier lifestyles supported by corporations (who are paying high premiums for health insurance) has begun!

The majority of the technological advances that bring efficiency to the delivery system require a commitment from the individual. That commitment could be time, effort, investment, or simply learning a technology—think Fitbit, iPad, calorie-counting applications, or simply logging into the individual patient portal that is used by your hospital. These tech-based health advancements enable us to have accountability. We can't count on others to keep us healthy. Thus, caring for oneself and technology become more critical—an area where millennials clearly have the advantage! While millennials no doubt feel picked on at times, they are more prepared for the incoming trends in healthcare delivery, which are rooted in technology and self-management.

Even with managed care being implemented to control costs, the current American delivery system is likely broken beyond repair, as health insurance has become unaffordable for the average American. As soon as employers realize that a growing number of their employees are willing to forego health benefits as they are unwilling to pay their share as a result of excessive cost, its likely more employers as a whole will begin to question why they continue to pay increased premiums each year as more services get cut.

Let me ask you a question: If you were in your mid-twenties and were told that 40 percent of your lifetime income would have to be allocated for your own personal healthcare expenses, would you be alright with it? Or would you say, "What if I live healthier, can we reduce that cost?" It's amazing what we can learn from millennial behavior, is it not?

Millennials have been raised in an era where self-management of one's personal health has been entrenched in the fabric of their upbringing. Since PPACA was passed in 2010, the majority of millennials, with the exception of those born between 1980-1985 (the X-ennials) will have little recollection of an era in which FFS was the model, diet and fitness were not a priority, and technology wasn't available at your fingertips 24/7 to assist individuals in making better decisions that affect personal health. This is because the cost of healthcare and paying for their own insurance is most often not a relevant topic until an individual graduates college and pays for it themself! All they know is the post-PPACA mentality. Now, it would be naïve to assume that the culture that will result from the drastic changes mandated by the PPACA is complete. Millennials are just young enough that the key cultural trends that emerge—the instant use of healthy technology and the importance of self-responsibility and management of one's health—are likely to be a core component of millennial thinking for their entire lives.

As described above, most millennials have only known an iPad, coordinated care, and instant connectivity for the majority of their post teen years. From a lifestyle perspective, the impression they will grow up with is technology that enhances their ability to make healthy decisions and better self-manage their own health. As a result, a healthier and more responsible society will evolve, and it is likely that these same individuals will see a rapid rise to leadership positions in the healthcare space.

While Gen Xers like myself have displayed a pattern of unhealthy issues, such as poor dietary choices and a lack of activity that led to problems associated with obesity, as millennials become the target of Madison Avenue, technology that enables healthy decisions in real time is available, affordable, and accessible to everyone. As a result, it has become much easier to make healthy decisions. Thus, dietary habits are improving, and fitness is becoming more of a priority.

There is a strong likelihood that Gen Xers had just enough exposure to the FFS era that we are too jaded to fully understand and pioneer the necessary change to a value-based, patient-centered model. Think about it. The two models are in direct contrast to each other, and experienced healthcare executives fought the required change that was mandated by the PPACA out of basic human nature, if nothing else. Everyone resists change, but when the change is a complete threat to everything you have ever been taught in your professional career? Yikes!

It's my belief that many healthcare organizations will skip over Generation X executives when looking for their leader of the future and look directly to a millennial who grew up knowing only technology, patient-centered care, and how to succeed in a value-based model. No bones in their body will resist the change! In fact, it's quite the opposite. An inherent excitement exists for being part of the transformation to a more humane model—patient-centered care. Should we consider the same approach in your business? Can you identify blockers (more seasoned or experienced executives) who might resist these new common societal trends, whereas a millennial executive would not?

Millennials grew up in an environment where creative technological approaches drastically changed delivery methods overnight in many industries, and healthcare delivery is no exception. In fact, healthcare is at the forefront. Millennials are much quicker to understand and adopt changes driven by technology than those who were trained in a FFS environment where keeping physicians happy was the main priority of the hospital operator. Millennials are no doubt positioned for success as future healthcare leaders. With this in mind, could your business benefit from this same type of approach? Could you benefit from a focus group of millennial employees making recommendations to improve culture and healthy lifestyles at your workplace?

Millennials embrace technological advances that improve health and reduce costs. In contrast, many of the holdover chief executives from the FFS era have fought technological implementation every step of the way as a way to control expenses and appease aging physicians. Aging physicians most often hold the few leadership positions in a hospital and are often uninterested in adapting to new practices in the twilight of their career. In fact, many physicians, whether they admit it or not, are threatened by technology, as in many cases it would reduce the need for a physician consult and, in turn, reduce the doctor's earning potential.

I saw this frequently as a CEO when dealing with cardiologists. While they would be impressed with updated technology, until someone taught them how to utilize it, what code to bill, and how much reimbursement they would receive for the procedure, the doctor had little interest in the hospital acquiring and implementing the technology, as without additional revenue being generated, the cardiologist often knew that the test result could eliminate the need for a patient to do a billable consult in his or her office.

In contrast, in my experience, millennial physicians, like the youngest of the Gen X physicians, are more likely to be focused on opting for a guaranteed salary and an employed position with 9 a.m. to 5 p.m. daily hours, as opposed to the traditional preference of becoming an independent physician. This has been a welcomed trend for integrated health systems like Kaiser Permanente and many national medical foundations, which utilize an employment model and have cash stockpiled to provide guaranteed security to these young doctors.

I was flipping through the *Orange County Register* daily newspaper one morning and saw a full-page "find a career" advertisement for a prominent local Indian casino in Southern California. Of the nine bullet points listed to attract potential candidates, six of them spoke to millennial values:

- Wellness health screenings

- Wellness seminars

- On-site fitness center

- Team member dependent scholarship program (for childcare or aging parents)

- Medical, dental, and vision insurance

- One free meal per day

There is a premium on millennial talent, and companies must identify the benefits that are attractive to millennial candidates to ensure that they are securing top talent. Millennial culture has been proven to promote healthy lifestyles and patient-centered care.

This chapter illustrates how physicians and seasoned executives in healthcare have turned their heads from technology for years, as it was contrary to their revenue model. It also showcased how financial incentives, bad habits, and the path of least resistance led to overutilization of healthcare services and resources, as well as institutionalizing patients in hospitals and nursing homes unnecessarily. As the emphasis shifts to self-management, personal engagement, and healthy lifestyles, the common traits of the millennial generation are in line to drive these initiatives in your workplace. This combination of recognition of bad habits and necessary cultural changes can lead to improved health for your employees and significant savings for your company.

With this in mind, Part I of this book explained the American healthcare affordability crisis and why the system is broken beyond repair. With this baseline understanding of the motivations and flaws in the current delivery system, you are now prepared to discover, in Parts II and III, the importance of consumer-driven healthcare, a Health-Wealth corporate culture, and nine steps that could save your company up to 30 percent annually on your healthcare spending. We wrap up Part I with three questions:

1. Are you prepared to embrace the characteristics associated with millennial culture that improve health and reduce healthcare spending?

2. Are you prepared to infuse a culture of self-accountability, self-management, and living a healthy lifestyle into your corporate culture?

3. Are you ready to declare on behalf of your company that you have reached the Health-Wealth tipping point?

PART II

EMPLOYEE OWNERSHIP OF HEALTHCARE DECISIONS AND SPENDING

YOUR CARRIER SENDING YOU a corporate premium increase notice each year has become as certain as the Internal Revenue Service calling upon you each April. The time has come to fight back.

This book was written for large employers who are ready to take control of the healthcare inflation situation. Did you know that current estimates show that at least 40 percent of a millennials' lifetime earnings in America will go to healthcare? If your carrier continues to increase your rates more than 5 percent a year, your company may not even survive long enough to see what percentage of a Gen Zer's income will have to go toward healthcare costs!

For American businesses, managing healthcare spending is a critical component of their overall business expenses, and the common tactic in recent years of company's going self-insured to control overall costs is no longer enough. It's just one small step. It's just the beginning.

Large corporations traditionally turn a blind eye to hyperinflating healthcare costs, as a competitive health insurance package is a critical recruiting tool to ensure top talent joins the organization. While that was definitely true with boomers and Gen Xers, corporations who still think that way are throwing money into the wind without cause. Sophisticated Gen X executives and millennials understand that competitive healthcare means a specialized offering with multiple choices, as described in this book.

Part II of this book provides an explanation of how important consumer-driven healthcare and establishing a Health-Wealth organizational culture have become. Part III of the book is a summary of nine steps for your company to consider to take back control of the situation. Beyond payroll and benefits, healthcare costs are likely your second or third largest expense. Yet to date, your organization has been helpless to manage these increased costs. It stops now.

A few words of caution before proceeding: It's critical that when you finish reading, you complete the online **Health-Wealth Loss Assessment** before jumping into any of these tactics. Many of these tactics are very specialized, and the assessment was designed to help steer you directly to those that provide the most opportunity for your organization, as well as the provider most likely to ensure success in partnering with your organization. A small portion of the online **Health-Wealth Loss Assessment** is included at the end of the book, but the complete assessment is available online at Health-Wealth. com/Loss-Assessment.

Your organization's Health-Wealth journey begins here.

CHAPTER 5

CONSUMER-DRIVEN MODELS AND TACTICS ARE ESSENTIAL

IMAGINE CAR SHOPPING for your daughter. You do all the research at home and decide on the exact car you want, down to every specific detail. Then, you head downtown with your daughter, full of excitement, seeking the best deal you can find on a safe new car for the most cherished aspect of your life. When you arrive on Auto Plaza Drive, you discover that the car you are looking for is offered by multiple dealerships. There are two new car lots, one on each side of the street, each with a separate owner. The exact car you decided on is offered on each lot, down to the very last detail—the same name brand, same color, and the same upgrades on both lots.

There is only one difference: the price. On the left side of the street, the car is listed at $16,000. On the right side of the street, it's listed at $42,000.

Why would anyone pay for the $42,000 car when they knew they could save more than 50 percent? The answer is that they might buy from the more expensive lot if they were paying with someone else's money and had no skin in the game.

When consumers spend other people's money without consequence, they are more likely to consider opting for the more expensive option—even if the products are identical—than they would be if it were their own money. That's just human nature. It's the same game in healthcare.

Welcome to the world of American healthcare! Employees and family members who are free to choose providers without any financial consequence will do exactly that.

Before proceeding, let's clarify the difference between fully insured companies and self-insured. Traditionally, businesses were fully insured and contracted with insurance companies to gain access to preferred rates. Employers then agreed to pay up to a maximum amount, and passed on a portion of that amount to employees via monthly premiums, deductibles, and co-payments/co-insurance.

Employers then would work with employees to manage costs and spending, but the amount they agreed to pay the insurer was set so they did not get to share in the savings. After years of annual premium increases, employers started to realize that the system was setup in a manner that the insurer would justify a rate increase each year with little room for the employer to reduce costs.

Employers started recognizing this was a system doomed to break them financially in the long run, so many made the decision to self-insure their health plans. While self-insurance puts a larger portion of the financial risk on the employer, they realized they could save money each year by controlling the costs associated with delivering healthcare to their employees.

The percentage of companies with self-insured health plans has been increasing since the mid-1990s. The number of companies with 500 or more employees who were self-insured increased from 71.6 percent in 1996 to 80.4 percent in 2015.

Seeing that many of the companies that have actively started managing healthcare expenditures have already converted to self-insured models, much of this chapter discusses tactics that are more effective in self-insured models than fully insured models. However, each of the tactics and steps discussed in this book will effectively help an organization improve health and reduce spending when implemented effectively.

For example, when an employee is having an elective procedure and is asked to choose a provider, the two closest hospitals might fit the following description: Hospital A is a reputable hospital twelve miles from the employee's home, and Hospital B is a reputable hospital one mile from home. The employee is asked to make a decision that bears no financial consequence to them or their family, as their copayment is identical at each facility.

There is a difference for the employer covering the patient, however. The price for the procedure at Hospital A is $16,000, while the price for the exact same procedure, often with the same exact doctor, at Hospital B is $42,000.

Similarly, when employees need a specific procedure and have already hit their maximum out-of-pocket, they quit caring what it costs the company, and that cost can have a variance of $20,000 or more. This is why many employers have started charging employees 10 percent of costs above their maximum, and doubling the employees' out-of-pocket minimum if they do not use a center of value. And guess what? It has worked. Employees are now paying attention.

"Many companies use tactics like this when attempting to steer employees from a costly service to less-costly one without sacrificing quality of care," said Ryan Miller, Director of Sales and Marketing for Centennial, an Alera Group Company. "An oft-used strategy is increasing the emergency room visit co-payment as a deterrent, which incentivizes the employee to choose urgent care, making the visit more cost effective for the employee and employer."

Employee abuse of the group health plan will typically cost the employer in one of two ways. Here are two examples:

- If the employer has a fully insured health plan, all the expenses of the current year will have some impact on the insurance renewal rate. This will not be a direct correlation (ie: $1,000,000 claim costs the group $1 million the following year), but it could create a larger increase in rates than normal the following year. So buyer beware.

- If the employer has a self-insured plan, the current year expenses will be paid directly by the employer up to their stop loss cap. A stop loss cap is the pre-arranged maximum cost an employer is financially responsible for, and any amount exceeding that cap is paid through stop-loss insurance policy.

The point here is that your employees are spending your money without consequence because the employee's financial responsibility is capped, while the employer's is not. This chapter will discuss tactics to change your employees' mind-set to take a much larger interest in the financial impact of their healthcare-related decisions. This concept is known as *consumer-driven healthcare*. Oftentimes, consumer-driven plans are referred to as *high-deductible plans*. While this is true in some cases, there are significant benefits to the plans as well.

The chart below illustrates the vast differences in prices in the Boston market, representing as much as 1,009 percent variance in prices between one provider and another, as well as a variance in excess of $9,600 for a rotator cuff repair. Similar examples can be cited from all over the country that illustrate the fact that hospital pricing is not based at all on a cost structure; it is just continual, year-over-year hyperinflation without any justification or evidence of increased costs. It's just lip service from the hospitals and old-school negotiating tactics to get employers to pay more, as that's always been the trend.

WILD VARIATIONS IN HEALTHCARE "DISCOUNT" PRICES

(negotiated discount, same procedure, different providers)

PROCEDURE	BOSTON (ZIP 02108) (50-MILE RADIUS)		
	Low	High	Variation
Chest X-ray	$32	$323	1,009%
Cholesterol Screening	$12	$153	1,275%
Emergency Dept. Visit	$129	$1,564	1,212%
Nuclear Stress Test	$600	$3,055	509%
MRI Lower Joint	$470	$2,056	437%
Rotator Cuff Repair	$2,536	$12,140	478%
Thyroid Stimulating Hormone	$14	$169	1,207%
Diagnostic Colonoscopy	$665	$2,593	390%
Ultrasound, Neck	$144	$640	444%

Source: Insurance Claims Data, MMS Analytics Proprietary Algorithms, Copyright © 2017 MyMedicalShopper

Until the turn of the millennium, most companies offered generous health insurance plans. Individual employee responsibilities were most often annual deductibles under $500 and 20 percent copay. When benefits are this strong, there is little incentive for the employee to be motivated to make educated choices on healthcare. It was initially viewed as simply shifting costs from the employer to the employee but has proven to be so much more. Consumer-driven methodologies can significantly reduce spending on healthcare for both the employer and employee, and overall employee health will improve as well. By the time PPACA passed, more than half of the employers in America were already implementing consumer-driven tactics or policies.

While consumer-driven healthcare can require significant start-up or transition costs for the employer, often exceeding $3,000 per employee (depending on the number of employees in your company), your organization will see a reduction in employee turnover within the initial eighteen months and a significant boost in employee morale. Additional new costs associated with offering consumer-driven plans may include plan administrative fees and contracting with new vendors to administer the plans properly.

Whether you are completely new to the concept of consumer-driven healthcare or converted to the model in prior years, this book and chapter will have plenty more tactics to consider adding to your arsenal to eliminate wasteful healthcare spending. Your company's financial well-being depends on it!

For those who have already converted to an employee-driven model, it's no longer enough to simply say you converted; you need to continually look to implement more tactics. Each year, additional consumer-driven tactics are identified that encourage employee engagement in healthcare decision making. It's important that your company continue to implement as many of these tactics as possible that make sense for your organization.

HOSPITAL PRICING TRANSPARENCY (OR LACK THEREOF) DIRECTLY AFFECTS THE EMPLOYER

Have you ever asked yourself why certain hospitals can charge outrageous, unjustifiable prices for the same procedure offered at more than 60 percent less across the street? The answer is because they can, and the American commercial health insurance model to date was conducive to allowing this laissez-faire approach by those with insurance. This lack of accountability from the individual employee has played a major role in driving up your company's healthcare costs.

Most hospitals refuse to post prices and will not even make them available when requested to do so by the patient. And the doctor is even more disconnected and unaware of the hospital prices. That's exactly how the hospital wants it. There is no transparency in hospital pricing. Likewise, there is no consumer accountability to prevent this behavior, so hospitals continue to raise prices year over year.

One of the hidden secrets of hospitals is that they consistently impose significant increases annually on high-volume procedures and impose smaller increases on lower-volume procedures. Thus, the number of total procedures that have rate hikes each year may be small, but profits increase as a result of the increases impacting the high volume procedures.

Interestingly, there is no evidence to date that a correlation between price and quality exists in healthcare. However, similar to the car business, there is a correlation between volume of procedures done and quality. The more cars a dealership sells, the higher the customer satisfaction. Likewise, the more surgeries a doctor does, the higher the quality. Thus, a key indicator of quality in many cases would be to identify the doctor or provider who completes the highest volume of the specific procedure you are seeking.

The American Hospital Association (AHA), the hospitals' lobbying body, and the AMA, the physician lobbying body, are two of the most powerful lobbying organizations in the country. Much like the unions, the AHA and AMA have long been known for making significant campaign contributions that have, in part, allowed this price gouging of the American public to continue. There has been little legislative push-back on the cost of healthcare, even though rates have doubled at least two to three times since 2000. The national healthcare debate has nothing to do with reducing costs, and as a result there is presently no momentum to force providers to be transparent and publish prices, which would in turn force competition.

The political healthcare debate is simply one of cost shifting and redistribution of wealth. The discussion in Washington is masked as a conversation rooted in affordability, but the topic of controlling hospital prices is not at all part of the conversation. The debate is simply focused on who ultimately will

> *The debate is simply focused on who ultimately will pay for these outrageous hospital prices: the individual who consumes the services, or the American taxpayer? It's simply a debate of cost shifting, and it such a passionate debate that it serves as the perfect distraction for elected officials to avoid being called out on the fact that there is little pressure being put on hospitals to both reduce prices and post them regularly.*

pay for these outrageous hospital prices: the individual who consumes the services, or the American taxpayer? It's simply a debate of cost shifting, and it such a passionate debate that it serves as the perfect distraction for elected officials to avoid being called out on the fact that there is little pressure being put on hospitals to both reduce prices and post them regularly. On the insurance side, while slow to do so, many insurers (including Anthem) publicly post a significant number of prices for procedures and include associated physician fees as well.

HEALTH-WEALTH PROVIDER TRANSPARENCY INITIATIVE

One of the objectives of Health-Wealth is to seek hospitals that voluntarily agree to post their prices online and agree to update them annually. It is only at the local level, through your company and other employers, that hospitals will be held accountable to post prices and feel the pressure to do so.

Thus, your company should write a letter to all local hospitals requesting that they share their prices with you annually and publish online. Make sure the letter states that the pricing sheet should include the complete charges associated with each procedure, including physician components and any other carved-out ancillary charges that are not included in the stated procedural rate.

The more companies that engage in consumer-based healthcare and create a corporate culture of responsibility, the more likely hospitals are to feel the competition and respond by being transparent. Let's get the ball rolling and create competition among hospitals.

MAKING THE CASE FOR CONVERSION TO A FULLY CONSUMER/EMPLOYEE-DRIVEN HEALTHCARE MODEL

The key argument in leading a company to convert to a consumer-driven approach is quite simple and impactful: the financial well-being of the company and all employees is at stake due to the rapidly rising cost of healthcare. It's the only uncontrollable cost the business faces each year, and it's increasing at an alarming rate. Job security is at risk for all if a change is not made!

Consumer-driven healthcare forces the employee to join the employer in forcing competition and transparency in the market. In short, consumer-driven healthcare forces employees to get skin in the game. It's as simple as that.

We have all heard the statistics that approximately 10 percent of employees account for more than half the of a company's total healthcare expenses, and to take it even further, it's often true that as low as 1 percent of your workforce and its dependents account for more than 25 percent of your company's entire healthcare spend. One of the key strategies in consumer-driven healthcare is to rein in those high utilizers.

Need more evidence of the trend in converting to consumer-driven plans? Most major hospitals and insurers started converting to consumer-driven plans between 2005 and 2010. Is that not the most obvious proof that consumer-driven healthcare is the most efficient means to healthcare savings for your company?

Critics suggest consumer-driven healthcare is just a means to shift costs from the employer to the employee. While there may be some truth to that, those employees who engage are able to have more control over their personal health and wealth.

We have yet to discuss the issue of consumer trust when it comes to complying with trusted expert's advice. In healthcare, that expert is one's personal doctor's advice regarding which hospital is ideal for care. Patients' commitment to utilizing the facility their doctor recommends is one of the biggest obstacles in getting employees to take ownership of the financial component of the provider decision. Doctors are now often employed by a health system or at a minimum financially incentivized by a system. Thus, doctors almost always refer patients to the system they are affiliated with, regardless of price. In most cases, the doctor has no idea what the cost to the patient and insurer is at each hospital, or the difference in price between two facilities. The expense to the patient and insurer is simply not the priority of the doctor.

While many companies have already ventured toward consumer-driven care, this chapter includes a comprehensive list of tactics that very few companies have implemented across the board. The tactics that are included are specific to each company. Factors affecting each individual company's choices include size of company, geography, access, demographics, and provider networks, among others.

STEPS TO IMPLEMENTING A CONSUMER-DRIVEN MODEL

Ultimately, each of the tactics your company implements should incentivize the employees to join the employer in forcing competition and transparency in the market. When employees embrace this consumer-driven approach, the result is a financial win for both the employer and the employees and, more often than not, improved health and employee satisfaction. The goal should be to implement as many as conceivable to reduce spending and improve health.

This chapter will begin by detailing some critical steps in adopting a consumer-driven model and will also provide a detailed list of other tactics to research and consider in preparing your plan.

Before preparing a conversion plan for your company, the first step is to complete the **Health-Wealth Loss Assessment**. Be conscious of the fact that not all of the tactics listed are a good fit for every company. In fact, without completing the **Health-Wealth Loss Assessment**, implementing these tactics can actually be extremely costly to your organization and may not provide any savings at all.

Once the various tactics to consider have been introduced, we will then discuss the importance of how the conversion takes place, including communication, a roll-out plan, and a support system to ensure long-term success. Many companies have successfully recouped their entire financial liability on the conversion within the first twelve months. This is most often the result of an extremely effective roll-out plan and support system.

CENTERS OF VALUE

One of the first steps in converting to a consumer-driven healthcare model is identifying "centers of value," or "centers of excellence." Centers of value are simply high-quality hospitals and doctors who are willing to share prices and lower rates to form a partnership with the employer and insurer. There are plenty of them out there, as many have struggled financially and in essence been forced to the bargaining table to re-capture or maintain market share, so they are anxious for you to engage them in this conversation. These centers of value are the pillars on which your consumer-driven model is built. Your organization cannot be successful without these critical partners in place.

Employers are more frequently referring employees to centers of value, specifically for high-cost procedures including hip replace- nt, back surgery, fertility, and bariatrics. In 2013, Walmart and al other major employers went so far as to contract with only four hospitals nationwide to serve as centers of excellence to perform free hip and knee replacements. Employees could still choose local providers, but then they would have to pay for the procedure themselves.[4] In fact, in 2017, almost 50 percent of Walmart's employees' hip replacement surgeries were performed at centers of value, up from approximately 40 percent in 2016. The point here is simple: price matters, and quality care is available at centers of value.

EMPLOYEE ENGAGEMENT

Empower employees to respectfully challenge and question care recommendations made by doctors and other clinicians, to solicit specific details on why they are making the recommendation, and to ask what the other options might be. For example, these are some questions your employees should feel empowered to ask:

- Why this hospital?

- Is that the only test I will need to determine the problem?

- What are my other options?

- What are the risks of not following through?

- Is there a generic drug that might be more cost efficient and equally effective?

- Would I be able to avoid another appointment if I am willing to self-administer or take some preventive steps on my own?

Most importantly, give your employees the encouragement and confidence to challenge the differences in the available options, including hospitals and ancillary providers (imaging, lab), and how

---

4 "NBGH/Optimum: Culture of Health Study," National Business Group on Health, accessed Novemeber 28, 2017.

their pricing structures differ. Also, remind them to investigate the cost of the complete episode of care, not just the procedure (in hospitals there are almost always separate invoices from physicians and ancillary service providers).

Even after the hospital stay concludes, when it comes to therapy and rehabilitation, employees should ask at every step of the way, "Do I need a doctor, nurse, or therapist to help me complete this activity, or can it be done on my own?" The savings can often be $100 an hour if you can self-administer. Once your employees have the confidence to engage at this level, you are on the path to success, as the employees have begun the journey of taking increased ownership in their personal health decisions!

A key step in getting the employee to engage in the process is obviously the personal financial commitment. The free healthcare option may be more tempting for a majority of employees (the incentive to choose the high-deductible plan is there is no annual premium or monthly payroll withheld from the employee) if the monthly individual component exceeds $50.

EMPLOYEE FINANCIAL CONTRIBUTION CHANGES

Another initial step in converting to a consumer-driven model is making significant changes to the employer and employee financial contributions. As you consider your strategy, keep in mind that historically, incentives have been much more effective than penalties, but both should be considered.

One incentive, for example, would be an employer lowering premiums significantly and voluntarily allocating approximately 50 percent of the reduced amount into a personal HSA for each employee. Thus, if a company lowered annual premiums by $2,100 and allocated $1,000 into the employee's HSA, it would offer significant incentive for the employee to convert from a traditional plan. In turn, the company would increase the out-of-pocket from $500 to $1,000 and increase coinsurance from 20 percent to 30 percent. This plan was very attractive to employees, as they not only save $1,100 out of the gate but also have an additional $1,000 to spend right off the bat—a potential savings of $2,100.

Remember, the savings to the company can be in excess of $20,000 for a single procedure due to the variance in prices, even after picking up these costs for the employee. Now that we have used the example of the car dealer, let's use a true healthcare example (see accompanying chart, as well) with the deductibles and coinsurance from the previous paragraph:

PRIOR MODEL

One of your employees is having an elective procedure. Let's assume an employee's first procedure of the year was an elective surgical procedure costing $10,000. Under the pre-consumer-driven plan, there was little motivation for employees to engage and shop. The company would have paid $7,500, and personal employee expenses would be $500 out of pocket and coinsurance of $2,000 (0.20 x $10,000), for a total employee cost of $2,500.

NEW, HIGH-DEDUCTIBLE, CONSUMER-DRIVEN MODEL *WITHOUT* EMPLOYEE ENGAGEMENT

In a consumer-driven model, at the beginning of the year the employee may have opted for the "high-deductible plan," and now they have the opportunity to research and reap the benefits of doing so. For this exact same procedure, the employee now has two choices. If the patient were to simply go to his or her favorite local hospital (Hospital A), the price is still $10,000, so they would pay a $1,000 deductible and $3,000 (0.30 x $10,000) coinsurance payment. So, the total would be $4,000, and the employee would exhaust the HSA of $1,000, for a final out-of-pocket bill of $3,000. The employer would pay the balance of $6,000.

NEW, HIGH-DEDUCTIBLE, CONSUMER-DRIVEN MODEL *WITH* EMPLOYEE ENGAGEMENT

In turn, if the employee were given information on competition in the local market and chose a center of value offering the same procedure at $4,000 instead of $10,000, the bill would look more like this: a $1,000 deductible and $1,200 (0.30 x $4,000) coinsurance payment. So, the total would be $2,200, and the employee would exhaust the HSA of $1,000 for a final out-of-pocket cost to the employee of $1,200. This represents a savings of $1,800 for the employee. That's no small potatoes for one procedure.

The company cost would also be significantly less, totaling $1,800. That's a savings of $5,700 over the pre-consumer-driven plan, and more than $4,200 was saved by simply choosing the center of value.

Don't forget that this same employee already saved $1,100 on the premium earlier in the year when they chose to convert to the consumer-driven (high-deductible) plan. This savings was a result of the multiple incentives motivating the employee to engage. In this example, the company's initial expense from lowering the annual premium by $2,100 has already been fully recouped, as the savings on this single example were $5,700.

It's that simple. The employer wins either way in the new model, as the costs dropped $1,500 even if the employee does not engage and a whopping $5,700 when the employee does engage by choosing a center of value.

	Prior Model	New, High-Deductible, Consumer-Driven Model without Employee Engagement	New, High-Deductible, Consumer-Driven Model with Employee Engagement
Procedure Cost	$10,000 (Hospital A)	$10,000 (Hospital A)	$4,000 (Hospital B)
Employee Out-of-Pocket	$500	$1,000	$1,000
Employee Coinsurance for Procedure	$2,000 (0.20 x $10,000)	$3,000 (0.30 x $10,000)	$1,200 (0.30 x $4,000)
Employee HSA	None	$1,000	$1,000
Total Employee Spend	$2,500	$3,000	$1,200
Employee Savings (Loss) Compared to Prior Model	N/A	($500) * Appears to be cost shifting, as employee did not participate in the savings	$1,800 * Evidence that the new model is NOT cost shifting when employee participates
Total Employer Spend	$7,500	$6,000	$1,800
Employer Savings Compared to Prior Model	N/A	$1,500	$5,700

This chart assumes the annual employee premium remains the same in each model

So now that we have given two examples, the question is this: How do we motivate our employees to put as much effort into researching and selecting a hospital as they do when they are buying a car?

Most industries are required to provide a detailed list of all required services to the consumer in advance of providing the service. Some industries even require the consumer to sign an extra form that says they understand what was disclosed to them. Why is it the opposite in healthcare? The provider is asking the consumer to prove their ability to pay yet is unwilling to provide and information about services necessary and associated pricing. It's almost laughable how hospitals have turned the tables on consumers, hidden prices, and used scare tactics to collect.

Often, hospitals tell you the cost of a procedure but do not include the ancillary costs or physician component in that quote. Yet when the invoice arrives in the mail, it's expected to be paid in full. In other industries this would be called a bait-and-switch and would be unethical and often illegal. But not in the hospital industry, consumers have little recourse to challenge the costs, if the invoice is actually even accurate—invoices are often inflated.

So I ask again, what are you going to do about this on behalf of your company? In consumer-driven healthcare, organizations must identify incentives that are strong enough to drive employees to prioritize healthcare decisions and become conscious consumers of healthcare services.

ON-SITE CLINIC

Opening an on-site clinic is one tactic that makes sense for most ̖anies with a corporate headquarters housing a significant ̖n of their workforce. This clinic can then house three or four employees whose entire focus is the health and wellness of your workforce. This might include nurses, case managers, or simply customer service team members to assist employees.

NURSE NAVIGATOR/HIGH-RISK CASE MANAGER

Remember when we discussed that approximately 10 percent of employees account for more than half the of a company's total health-care expenses? Here is a direct solution to reduce that spending. A nurse navigator or case manager is a company-sponsored or employed navigator assigned to work with and manage the health of employees identified as high-risk. These employees volunteer for the program, which is a positive sign as they are proactively engaging in the process. There are, of course, incentives to volunteer for the program, as the company pays through the nose for those employees with chronic conditions who choose not to engage and manage the chronic issue on their own. These incentives can be additional paid days off, $100 gift cards, or a number of other valued incentives.

Its best to "contract" with the nurse navigator as many employees are still hesitant to share their personal health information with their employer. Thus, implementing a model ensuring independence between the nurse navigator and your company is critical.

MEDICAL TOURISM

Guess what? Your company's center of value may be in Costa Rica, India, Las Vegas, or the county just to the south of your business headquarters? Why? Because the complete cost of all-inclusive care could be less than $15,000, instead of $80,000 at your local provider. How is this possible? Well, we have covered that in detail. There is no accountability or justification in hospital pricing in the United

States. Each hospital sets its own rates, and the variance is significant. There is no reason to believe any accountability is on the horizon, either. Hospitals, surgery centers, and independent practices have the ability to set their own rates and charge significantly less than many larger hospitals, which is why medical tourism can exist even from one county to the next. If you don't shop, you will never know.

Thus, the opening of many new medical tourism focused companies abroad is just one sign that medical tourism has seen explosive growth in in the last ten years. Medical tourism continues to grow in popularity, as the average cost of care can be drastically cheaper by simply getting on an airplane and traveling to a destination. Consider this: the employer pays for airfare and four nights' accommodations for an employee and one guest, then covers the cost of care. Using the example cited earlier, with a $5,000 travel budget for the employee and guest plus a $15,000 all-inclusive procedure, the employer's total spend is $20,000, in comparison to $60,000 or $80,000 had the employee received the care locally, even if they had chosen a local center of value. Even after travel expenses, the company often saves more than 50 percent of the potential cost.

Medical tourism can even refer to the town next door, not just the other side of the globe. If you think about it, this concept of going out of market, whether just a few miles or thousands of miles, is completely backwards. The local providers have the complete ability to lower costs and compete, they just don't have any financial incentive to do so, so they continue to raise prices aggressively.

Because American employees have been slower to acclimate to international medical tourism than employers had hoped, many employers have simply looked to the next town to find a hospital that will partner with them to be a center of value. Referring back to the employee savings in the example earlier in the chapter, how many of your employees would be willing to drive an extra forty to sixty minutes for a procedure if it saved them $1,800 or more? If the employer provides resources illustrating that the quality outcomes and patient satisfaction at the out-of-market provider are equal or better, my guess that the answer is that almost all of your employees would choose to drive the extra hour for the procedure.

In 2017, Santa Barbara County in California announced it was going to take all of its hip surgeries to San Diego County, a three-hour drive to the south. This decision was not driven by a shortage of doctors or hospitals in Santa Barbara; in fact, Cottage Health in Santa Barbara has multiple hospitals and a great reputation. Apparently, the county was able to negotiate a significant discount by shopping the contract out of the county. Once they showed the employees that the quality scores were just as strong at the other hospital, as well as how much less the employee would pay in their share of cost, the program was an easy sell.

The employer could also incentivize the behavior by offering to pay for all of the employee's out-of-pocket costs, including the deductible and coinsurance. Additionally, the savings to the company are so great that the employer should also consider paying for travel and accommodations if the provider is more than forty minutes from the workplace.

CONTROLLING PHARMA COSTS THROUGH CONSUMER (EMPLOYEE) BEHAVIOR

In my experience, the average company will spend 10 to 22 cents per dollar of healthcare spending on pharmaceutical costs. There are many steps that can be taken to rein in pharmacy spending. The following are three tactics that can significantly reduce company and employee spending on medications:

- Make generic drugs completely free to your employees. There is a huge savings opportunity here!

- Contract out your company's pharmaceutical purchasing to a pharmacy benefit manager to create competition.

- Empower your employees to ask for generics or alternatives to high-priced drugs.

First, make generic drugs completely free to your employees. Doctors are being paid significant amounts of money by pharmaceutical companies to recommend high-cost drugs. Hospitals often have much higher margins on the name-brand dugs they provide, as well. And now, even insurers are being incentivized in the same manner to eliminate generic drugs and force your company and your employees to pay for name-brand drugs. Just say no! Over-communicate the importance of this tactic as a huge potential for personal savings.

Second, by bidding out your company's pharmacy purchasing to a pharmacy benefit manager, you will create competition for your business and drive costs down. Simply doing a request for proposal (RFP) and trying to manage your own costs no longer makes sense, as, in my experience, pharma can often be up to 20 percent of your overall healthcare costs. Drug costs should be as much a priority as the remainder of your healthcare spending, as it accounts for one of every five dollars that you and your employees spend on healthcare. Your employees have the power to drive significant savings on pharma. Most companies now have access to no-copay generic drugs at Walmart, Target, and other retailers, or even an inexpensive mail-order option. While these are all attractive options as an employer, best to hire a benefit manager to analyze which approach or approaches are most suitable for your organization's needs. Completing a **Health-Wealth Loss Assessment** will assist in identifying an appropriate pharmacy benefit manager for your organization.

Third, empower your employees to engage. It may feel like this is a common theme. Here is why it sounds familiar: consumer-driven healthcare relies on the consumer to engage. Your conversion will not be successful without employee engagement. This is never truer than in simply empowering patients to ask the doctor if there is an alternative to a high-priced drug. I personally have found that even after I've asked doctors if there was an appropriate generic, they did not communicate a suitable alternative to me—but the pharmacist did. Determined to be an engaged consumer, I had the pharmacist call the doctor and request permission for an order to switch to the generic. You would be amazed how pharma companies have brainwashed doctors to incentivize them to prescribe expensive medications to patients.

ADDITIONAL CONSUMER-DRIVEN HEALTHCARE TACTICS TO CONSIDER

This is a list, in no specific order, of tactics to consider employing in your organization as you convert to a consumer-driven mind-set:

- Make wellness and preventive procedures free to employees; consider offering them on-site annually.

- As part of your pre-op consultation, proactively steer employees to a center of excellence by identifying the similar quality and significant savings.

- Reduce the employee's cost for a routine doctor's office visit to as low as possible ($30 or less) to keep them more attractive than the emergency room or a twenty-four-hour clinic. The key is early detection of illness.

- Increase the employee portion of an emergency room visit to a minimum of $500.

- Offer no employee copay for certain procedures when they choose a center of excellence (the savings to the employer could be in excess of $20,000).

- Double the employee's out-of-pocket costs if an employee chooses NOT to go to a center of value. The company could even take the aggressive position of simply not taking any financial responsibility if the employee chooses not to go to a center of value.

- As discussed earlier for specific procedures, when employees hit their maximum out-of-pocket, they quit caring what it costs the company, and that cost can have a $20,000 or more variance just on the company expense. Thus, consider charging the employee 10 percent of costs above their maximum, and double employees' out-of-pocket costs (deductibles, co-pays, and coinsurance) if they do not use a center of value.

- Make second opinions free for elective procedures. A $100 doctor's appointment could save the company thousands.

- For elective procedures, consider picking up the deductible and coinsurance costs for employees when they aggressively shop and it leads to significant savings.

- Offer employees a financial reward for identifying billing errors on medical bills. Reward the employee by paying them 50 percent of any money refunded to the employer by a hospital or insurer for billing errors.

- Approximately 64 percent of employers offer claims dispute assistance to employees, whether financial or simply providing support.[5]

- Make sure stop-loss insurance is in place to cover high-cost procedures. As expensive as it is, even one or two catastrophic cases per year, such as auto accidents, cancer, or other expensive cases, can throw your entire year's healthcare spending out of whack.

There are many tactics to employ in a consumer-driven model, and this chapter by no means represents a complete list. However, once your organization has completed the assessment and identified which tactics are likely to have the most significant impact on your organization, it will have the framework for adapting to, or continuing to evolve into, a consumer-driven model.

DEVELOPING A ROLL-OUT PLAN FOR CONVERTING TO OR INCREASING CONSUMER-DRIVEN TACTICS

Now that many of the tactics have been discussed, there are several keys to maintaining a consumer-driven culture. Most organizations introduce the consumer-driven model on a voluntary basis. However, as financial pressures increase and organizations see the benefits and savings of consumer-driven models, it is not uncommon for the company to drop all of its traditional plans and convert to an entirely consumer-driven model within a year of the voluntary launch.

---

5   "The Large Employers' Health Care Strategy and Plan Design Survey," National Business Group on Health, accessed November 28, 2017.

Once you have completed your assessment, identified the framework, and developed a formal plan, it is critical that a comprehensive roll-out plan is developed. The roll-out plan must be rooted in two very specific objectives:

- Identify the benefits of the conversion for the employee (and employer).

- Communicate these benefits clearly.

A communication strategy is critical when launching the initiative, so over-communicate! Use as many methods as possible to reach your employees and continue communicating the importance of this conversion for both the employee and the financial well-being of the employer. It's essentially a message of shared responsibility. If communicated effectively, the employee will learn that by engaging in the process, they will likely save significant money on unnecessary healthcare spending, and the company will as well. Reiterate that the employee will be rewarded in multiple ways for making these responsible decisions. Ultimately, your company needs to make this change, and the most important message that can be communicated is that, in addition to the employees' opportunity for significant savings on healthcare spending, the financial well-being and longevity of the organization (and thus, job security) depends in large part on the employees rallying behind this conversion and embracing it.

There is so much more to consumer-driven healthcare that it would be impossible to summarize it in one short chapter. You will find elements of a consumer-driven approach and culture in just about every one of the Health-Wealth Steps discussed in Part II of this book. The best way to identify which Health-Wealth Steps are the best fit for your organization is by completing the **Health-Wealth Loss Assessment**. Even if your organization converted to a consumer-driven model in prior years, this book will have plenty more offerings to consider adding to your arsenal of tactics to eliminate wasteful healthcare spending. Your company's financial well-being depends on it!

CHAPTER 6

CREATING A HEALTH-WEALTH CULTURE

IN 2015, I WENT FOR a routine physical and my lab results came back "pre-diabetic." What? I had never had problems like this before. "What does this even mean?" I asked. I went online and learned I needed to improve my diet and exercise more. So I made some changes and now live a healthier lifestyle. And it was not easy.

If employees engage and commit to living a healthy lifestyle, it will lead to less healthcare spending and increased wealth for the individual and employer. And not just financial wealth—Health-Wealth as well! The employee and the company will be healthier all around, and the company as a whole will see a healthy change in corporate culture.

I learned as a young executive that in business, you don't identify objectives without assigning them financially measurable outcomes. I employed that same approach in developing the nine steps, or tactics, for this book. Step 1 may be the exception. Although there will be a long-term measurable reduction in healthcare spending and potentially an increase in margin as a result of increased productivity and reduced loss time, measuring the financial impact of your team converting to a healthier lifestyle will not initially be simple.

However, it's critical enough that it still be included as one of the steps. And further, it is purposefully placed after Step 1: Alternative Insurance Models, because this change in culture is not just about making better diet and exercise decisions, but it's also about engaging in the consumer-driven healthcare process to manage your entire health.

Teach your employees that living a healthy lifestyle and reducing medical expenditures is a financial asset to them and their family, no different than owning a home. One employee implementing a personal Health-Wealth plan decreases healthcare spending for the individual, the company, and all other employees!

The goal for your organization is to empower and educate employees to commit to three critical steps that affect employee and employer Health-Wealth:

- Access personal health information to remain educated on needs.

- Develop a healthy living plan that can be electronically measured daily.

- Stay out of the hospital as much as possible!

When your employees are committed to these three priorities, you will achieve significant Health-Wealth savings.

FEDERAL SUPPORT

Both the Americans with Disabilities Act and Genetic Information Nondiscrimination Act address corporate wellness programs, and although they are legally required to be voluntary, each act allows employers to offer incentives to employees who voluntarily participate. Study these regulations and take advantage of them. Healthcare has a significant impact on your bottom line, and when the federal government offers financial support to encourage financially responsible behavior by your employees, it's definitely worth researching and implementing programs when appropriate.

START AT THE TOP

This conversion to a consumer model and Health-Wealth corporate culture will not happen without complete support and buy-in from the entire executive suite, particularly the CEO. These steps can only be achieved if company leadership, all the way to the top, walks the walk and engages. The CEO cannot brush off this conversion to consumer-driven care and a 24/7 healthy lifestyle. He or she must be an active, vocal, and visible participant, as should the remainder of the C-suite executives.

There should be specific activities in your roll-out plan that call for the CEO to participate or lead by example on a monthly basis. These activities should be high profile and planned to maximize exposure. A similar plan should be developed for all executives, whether it's captaining a walk team for a fundraiser, hosting the employee bike club, or leading healthy cooking classes periodically. These are all great activities for executives to participate in to reinforce that this transition in corporate culture starts at the top.

LAUNCHING AND COMMUNICATING

Once your leadership has bought into being highly involved in the process, it is imperative that leadership take an active role in constant and consistent communication that living a healthy lifestyle serves as a core value for your organization. The goal is to over-communicate the strategy. Tactics to consider implementing include the following:

- Hold a monthly, company-wide themed poster campaign.

- Post executive "quotes of the day" as a reminder to make healthy choices.

- Host a bimonthly breakfast with the CEO to answer questions and have corporate partners on-site to promote healthy living.

- Host "lunch and learns" and staff meetings to motivate them and share with them available resources to further engage.

- Include a healthy living quote or statement in the executives' e-mail signatures.

- Share a recipe of the week or month.

- Convert vending machines to healthy offerings, and eliminate soda machines.

- Utilize bulletin boards for enhanced communication.

- Develop a comprehensive employee portal on your company website and create an application to provide continual communication updates.

- Utilize newsletters, billboards, community partnerships, and department meetings.

- Do a monthly CEO newsletter.

- Conduct a direct mail campaign that will help appeal to the spouse or family member as well.

- Have a spouse and family education meeting or fair twice annually so family members take ownership as well.

- Have your insurance provider and preferred providers do periodic newsletters and communication pieces.

Each of these tactics should be included in your comprehensive launch plan when converting to a consumer-driven model in order to enhance your consumer-driven offering and establish a permanent Health-Wealth culture within your organization.

Equally as important as the launch plan is the maintenance communications plan. Establishing any sort of cultural change requires consistency and longevity. Consistent, monthly communication—both verbally and visually—is critical. Essential tactics include maintaining and sharing a monthly dashboard of key Health-Wealth indicators. Health-Wealth indicators could include, but are not limited to, the following:

- What percentage of employees chose the consumer-driven plan (if you still offer a choice)

- What percentage of employees chose centers of value for procedures month over month

- How much the company spent on out-of-pocket costs month over month and quarter over quarter

- Days without work related injuries or lost days due to work injury (for larger employers)

- Number of employees qualifying for a well-day off as a result of improved lifestyle and review the data year over year (see Incentives section later in this chapter)

- Average steps per day per employee

There are so many more indicators you can include. Have fun with it, but more important than fun, make sure you send a consistent message that the organization is committed to continuous improvement in each of these areas month over month!

THE MILLENNIAL EFFECT ON CREATING A HEALTH-WEALTH CULTURE

Most American companies have a head start on this conversion. It's likely that the lifestyle choices of the millennials they hire pertaining to diet, activity, and exercise are already healthier than those of their Gen X and boomer colleagues. It is imperative that your organization embrace and celebrate these healthy living habits so they become more infectious with your Gen X and boomer employees.

Further, the millennial generation is accustomed to having technology in their hands at all times. That technology has been entrenched in their lifestyle behaviors as well. This includes fitness apps, dieting apps, Fitbits, and other technology that contributes to their health. As millennials join your team on a larger scale, your company will experience a downward spending trend on healthcare and improved Health-Wealth culture. Thus, the more aggressive your organization can be in promoting this culture company-wide, the sooner the organization will begin to see measurable downward spending on healthcare.

THE ON-SITE CLINIC

As discussed in prior chapters, organizations with 2,000 or more employees located on one campus or within a few miles of each other should open an on-site clinic. This clinic will serve as much more than just a doctor's office. Just the fact alone that it is a doctor's office will encourage preventive and well-patient visits, reduce time lost to employees needing to drive to the doctor, and reduce procrastination in seeking care to avoid costlier services when an employee grows more ill. Perhaps the biggest financial victory with an on-site clinic is that it will reduce unnecessary emergency department usage.

Make that doctor free to employees.

If your organization does not have enough employees or the capital budget to operate a profitable clinic on your own, consider placing the clinic in a high-traffic consumer area and offer access to the community as well. This option is also very attractive to doctors who may consider being housed at the clinic. Also, only high-performing local doctors should be permitted to work in your on-site clinic.

Your clinic can have one or multiple doctors. Depending on the clinic structure that best fits your needs, it would be ideal to have a doctor and an NP, as NPs are much less expensive. Also, if you are able to afford both a doctor and an NP, it is recommended that your goal be that one of them is female and the other is male (it does not matter which one is the doctor and which is the NP). Having one individual of each gender on-site is the key to appeasing the cultural and religious sensitivity of all employees, as well as to making each of your employees as comfortable as possible.

While millennials are not likely to be as entrenched in this belief, be prepared for both your Gen X and boomer employees to complain about privacy issues when you first open your clinic.

Inevitably you will hear a fraction of your employees state that they are not interested in utilizing the on-site clinic, as "I don't want the whole world knowing about my personal life and health." For this reason, it is imperative that the doctor, NP, and staff be contracted workers and not actual employees of your organization. Over time, aging employees will grow as trusting as the millennials and realize that an individual's personal health information is required by law to stay personal—even to the employer!

TACTICS TO CREATE A HEALTH-WEALTH CULTURE

After you open a clinic, you have an entire new world of opportunities to consider. Most of these tactics would be most effective if managed from a central location, like the on-site clinic. So think of this section's nickname as "Accessorizing Your On-site Clinic to Create a Health-Wealth Culture."

For example, based on your organization's **Health-Wealth Loss Assessment**, many of the following tactics would be recommended to maintain a Health-Wealth culture:

- Refuse to hire smokers. Many companies no longer hire smokers. Imagine how much they are saving annually on their healthcare spending as a result. You can, too.

- For existing employees who smoke, charge an additional 25 percent for healthcare benefits.

- Convert to a completely smoke-free campus. They did this at every hospital I worked, at and it was successful. And at each hospital, everyone swore it would never work.

- Build an on-site fitness center.

- Hire nurse navigators, who are essentially case managers providing services to employees and specialized support for those with high-risk conditions. Even if there is no on-site clinic, create space on campus to provide these services.

- Contract with the following specialists to provide free or cheap consultations to your employees one day a week in the clinic or on-site gym:

  □ Registered dietitian

  □ Massage therapist (get local massage therapy students to do chair massages—they work for cheap!)

  □ Personal trainer

  □ Chiropractor

  □ Acupuncturist

  □ Diabetes coordinator

  □ Contract with an ergonomics expert to work closely with your chiropractor (or the chiropractor can do both)

- For a few hours a week, offer free consultations and coaching from your appointed Health-Wealth liaison in your human resources department for any employees interested in living a healthier lifestyle.

ANNUAL HEALTH-WEALTH ASSESSMENT

Consumer-driven plans increase premiums for employees and covered spouses who do not complete an annual physical exam. Further, your company should adjust the premium rate of each employee based on the employee's willingness to commit to a plan to address any risk areas identified during the annual physical exam. The better the health, the lower the premium. Requirements of the voluntary Personal Health-Wealth Annual Assessment for employees and spouses (they get an annual premium discount if they volunteer) include the following:

- Complete a physical exam with doctor

- Meet with company navigator or Health-Wealth designee

- Review any indicators or risk factors

- Set health goals for the year

- Doctor and employee sign the final document and retain a copy

PREMIUM ADJUSTMENT FOR EMPLOYEES ENGAGING IN THE HEALTH-WEALTH LIFESTYLE

Employee Participation	Employee Commitment	Annual Premium Adjustment	Sample Annual Premium
Traditional employer plan	None	Higher annual premium	$2,400 ($200 monthly)
Consumer model: voluntary annual exam, reduced premium option	Volunteer for annual physical exam	Regular annual premium	$1,200 ($100 monthly)
Consumer model: voluntary annual exam, reduced premium with plan and monitoring option	Volunteers for annual physical exam Volunteers for follow-up Health-Wealth lifestyle planning consult & monitoring	Lower annual premium	No annual premium

As part of your conversion to a consumer-driven model, each employee will be offered a free annual physical exam, and if they refuse, their premium will increase significantly. Employees can then supplement the physician meeting by agreeing to meet with the company human resources delegate to assess the "wealth" portion of their plan in an annual Health-Wealth assessment.

After reviewing employees' annual health assessments, the human resources Health-Wealth designee will assist them in identifying programs that the company makes available to improve health based on their individual situation. In these meetings, employees are made aware of services and incentives available to them to assist in committing to live a heathy lifestyle, either through qualifying for incentives, potentially including additional paid time off (PTO) days!

Your company should require the covered dependent (most often a spouse) to complete an annual physical exam as well. Organizations truly committed to converting to a Health-Wealth culture will offer a free annual Health-Wealth assessment.

CONCIERGE PROGRAM

Offer a company-specific concierge medicine program. Whether or not they operate an on-site clinic, larger employers are often offering a voluntary concierge physician benefit. This is a completely voluntary benefit and can be costly, but it is a premium service. Your company can contract with a doctor, preferably one who works in your on-site clinic, to provide 24/7 personal care and access to employees who enroll in the program. This doctor not only fulfills the traditional personal family physician role for employees who enroll but also agrees to answer his or her mobile phone 24/7 in addition to providing support services for wellness, prevention, chronic disease management, and living a healthy lifestyle.

Employees are under no obligation to join, but many will pay to join when they find out the doctor makes house calls, returns texts, and returns phone calls promptly! Guess what: if your employees opt in, they are actually paying to help you reduce your overall health costs! Touché!

Of all the tactics we discuss, this one could potentially yield your organization the most savings of all, and so long as enough employees participate, it may not even cost you a dime!

When you create your concierge program, target doctors who are already working in your on-site clinic. If the concierge physician does not work in your on-site clinic, require that he or she see patients in the on-site clinic at least two half-days a week. Many large organizations have found concierge programs to be one of the most valued benefits of employees who engage in the consumer-driven process—and they do it at their own expense!

CONVERTING HIGH UTILIZERS TO HEALTH-WEALTH SUCCESS STORIES

Now that we have discussed programs that all employees can benefit from, let's focus on reducing wasteful spending on our biggest utilizers of healthcare services. For example, in my experience an obese worker likely costs the employer, on average, more than $25,000 annually. The 80/20 rule is a baseline for employee health costs: Historically, less than 20 percent of employees, predominantly those with chronic conditions, likely make up from more than 80 percent of a company's overall health costs. As companies become more efficient, that number likely approaches the 90/10 rule, because those with chronic conditions will remain the most difficult to manage.

For this reason, it is essential that your company create programs for the high utilizers consuming the majority of your healthcare dollars. The first step in managing high utilizers is utilizing your navigators (case managers). Under the supervision of the nurse navigators, companies would be wise to develop disease management programs to support employees with high-cost, chronic diseases or symptoms including the following:

- Coronary disease

- High blood pressure

- Obesity

- Depression

- Asthma

- Diabetes

Also, provide support to all employees who are pre-diabetic or diabetic, and give them a bonus for meeting quarterly and adhering to their health plan. Consider other, similar disease-specific programs based on your company's greatest areas of need.

I've found that up to 20 percent of a company's employees could be affected by one of these high-cost, chronic diseases. There is much a company can do on the preventive side to assist these employees and family members in improving health, reducing symptoms, and living a Health-Wealth lifestyle. And as discussed before, this small percentage of employees make up the majority of your company's annual healthcare spending.

SUPPORT AND ACCESS FOR ALL EMPLOYEES

Most companies pay lip service to healthy lifestyles and wellness but don't provide the necessary access to employees. Human resources is often the contact sought out by employees, so give that department the resources to educate employees and fulfill their desire to live a healthy lifestyle.

Whether you choose to simply use your navigators for this role or assign separate Health-Wealth liaisons in your human resources department, these dedicated employees are critical. These individuals would be available one or two days a week in the cafeteria during lunch to answer questions and should have an open-door policy for meetings and walk-ins daily. They are there to service your employees, so make them available!

The main role of these individuals is to educate and steer your employees to centers of value when appropriate. Additional value-added services that complement your Health-Wealth culture include a free annual consultation on completing a medical advance directive for end-of-life wishes.

As it pertains to centers of value, these liaisons maintain and make available to employees quality data on local hospitals and doctors. This data often includes the following indicators of quality:

- For doctors:

    □ High volume

    □ Patient feedback

    □ Employee feedback—an internal Yelp!

    □ Healthgrades ratings

    □ Medicare comparison

- For hospitals:

- Medicare Star Ratings

- Patient feedback

- Employee feedback—an internal Yelp!

- Healthgrades ratings

Having access to this data makes the steering process much simpler, which increases your percentage of employees choosing centers of value. And remember, this is partially sales, so actively promote the data that best tells the story that your employees will save and get high quality at centers of value.

NUTRITIONAL CAMPAIGN

A true Health-Wealth culture is a campus focused on eating healthy. This means only healthy selections in vending machines and the cafeteria. If you have not done so already, phase out any foods, sodas, or snacks that are in direct contrast to your goal of a healthy workforce. If you have food trucks or vendors servicing your employees or sponsoring "lunch and learns," establish criteria for what food qualifies.

Geisinger recently removed all sugary drinks from its facilities in 2017. Sugary drinks can contribute to increased levels of obesity, type 2 diabetes, heart disease, and other issues.

Further, consider hosting a farmer's market on campus weekly, seek out a discount at health-focused grocery stores, and find incentives for your employees to buy and consume healthy foods. Complement these efforts with a poster campaign encouraging healthy eating and drinking, as well as weekly or monthly e-mails and newsletters focused on healthy eating, recipes, and meals.

INCENTIVES

Many companies nationwide have gone even one step further by offering financial savings as the key incentive in converting to a consumer-driven model and creating a Health-Wealth culture. While financial incentives have historically been more effective than penalties or fines, both can be effective. But positive reinforcement can go a long way in kick-starting the cultural change your organization is committing to.

Companies like Vitality have experienced rapid growth as a result of "gamifying" this emerging trend of healthy lifestyles. Employers have realized the significant money that can be saved on wasteful healthcare spending, so they contract with companies like Vitality to offer formal incentive programs for their workforce. These gamified programs digitally track and monitor your annual Health-Wealth lifestyle plan and reward progress and accomplishments by allowing the employee to choose from different prizes or gift cards.

Your **Health-Wealth Loss Assessment** will provide a good indicator as to whether or not a formal incentive program would be an appropriate cultural fit for your organization. If the assessment suggests that your company may not initially be a great candidate for a formal program, it will also provide details on steps that will likely move your organization closer to being ready for a commitment of that magnitude. Be cautious not to take on too much at once; some companies have fallen victim to this by signing with a formal incentive partner right out of the gate.

A key incentive for employees to convert is if the organization eliminates PTO for sick days altogether and replaces those days with PTO for "well days." What an incentive for an employee to commit to a healthy lifestyle!

This tactic is encouraged, as sick days actually serve as a reward for employees being ill. Employers should consider replacing sick days with "well" days off that can be earned by committing to a healthy lifestyle plan and sticking to the plan consistently. Thus, you can earn days off for being healthy, but do not get paid when you are feeling ill.

For example, give up to two additional paid days off per year for individuals achieving health lifestyle goals. The money spent on PTO for the limited number of employees who achieve the goals will be a fraction of the money saved as your corporate culture shifts to the Health-Wealth approach.

Creating an environment conducive to a successful consumer-driven health plan requires a workforce committed to a culture of healthy lifestyles. In this book, we refer to this as a "Health-Wealth culture." Although millennials as a whole are more conditioned to living a healthy lifestyle, it is imperative that American companies instill these same traits in members of the prior generation on their workforce. For a summary of the tactics in this chapter that will support this transition, refer to the list below:

- Ensure CEO and leadership engagement in the process.

- Over-communicate launch and reasons for launch by using multiple communication platforms.

- Embrace millennial culture.

- Accessorize your on-site clinic with multiple offerings.

- Tactics

  - Offer a free voluntary annual health assessment. Offer incentives to drive participation.

  - Offer a concierge program.

- Convert high-utilizers to success stories.

- Provide support and access for all employees.

- Offer plenty of incentives.

- Run a nutritional campaign.

- Reward those who are successful. Be sure to reward the biggest improvers, not the just the fitness fanatics! This is key for those whom others might not deem healthy, as you are rewarding improvement and success—not the healthiest person!

- Thank those who help make the culture infectious!

PART III

NINE STEPS TO
CORPORATE
HEALTH-WEALTH

OFFER ALTERNATIVE INSURANCE MODELS

WHILE MANY OF THE STEPS to Health-Wealth featured in this book are simple, singular concepts, Step 1 is more about taking a step back and exploring all insurance options available to employers and individuals. Aside from the traditional, well-known HMO, PPO, and exclusive provider organization (EPO) models offered through major health plans, the launch of the PPACA and employers being permitted to opt-out saw the reemergence of some long-standing alternative plans and brought about the birth of some new models, as well.

While the futures of specific initiatives introduced by Obamacare are often murky, employers will likely continue to have choices to offer employees when selecting healthcare benefits. Waivers allowing companies of a certain size or less to opt out of the mandate or provide employees with monthly pay "in lieu" of benefits may put those companies in a position to benefit from employees choosing to work directly with a co-op or alternative model, as described below. The growth in popularity of HSAs could open up the potential for employees to opt out of the company-sponsored plan and choose a faith-based co-op if they believe it will better fit their needs.

This chapter will discuss a few of the more common alternative options that have been growing in popularity in recent years and may be adaptable in your organization as a complement to or replacement for your traditional insurance plan. Below are descriptions of three models that have seen significant growth since the passing of the PPACA.

COST-SHARING COMMUNITY MODEL (CSCM): CSCMs are experiencing rapid growth, as they have proven to reduce costs for employers and families. CSCMs are designed to increase efficiency by utilizing technology such as mobile application scheduling, immediate virtual or telephonic access to clinicians and physicians for members, telehealth consults, and remote monitoring devices to ensure more efficient care delivery at a lower cost. One key benefit includes being able to choose whichever doctor you prefer—just be sure to confirm the fee structure for cash-pay patients with the doctor in advance.

Healthcare cost-sharing models have existed for more than twenty-five years, and membership for all plans combined is expected to surpass one million by 2018. CSCM combines the consumer-driven incentives of discounted value services with technological advances that allow more timely access and are much less expensive than traditional plans.

One example of a leading CSCM is Sedera Health. Sedera's members present themselves to medical providers as "self-pay patients." Sedera then assists in offsetting medical expenses that exceed $500 or $1,000 per episode, depending on membership level. Sedera's program offers a three-tiered approach: the Minimum

Essential Coverage level for preventive needs, an HSA, and health-care sharing for larger medical incidents. Sedera Health partners with Teladoc for telehealth and remote monitoring services and with 2nd.MD to guarantee timely access to physicians. Services include discounted surgeries, counseling, medical bill negotiation, appointment scheduling, reduced prescription costs, and physician searches. There is no copay to access 24/7 services from Teladoc, which serves an incentive for members to adapt to doing virtual consults. Many members find virtual consults to be extremely convenient, as they can do the consult from the comfort of their home or workplace.

FAITH-BASED COST-SHARING MODEL: Another form of an alternative cost-sharing model is a faith-based cost-sharing program. Members of a faith-based community pay into the ministry, and monthly fees are applied to other members' medical bills. This is not an insurance product. Members are often required to commit to live the standards of the group or church, including praying for other members, abstaining from sexual immorality, and not using illegal drugs.

Coverage for preexisting conditions is limited, abortions are not covered, and preventive care, routine prescriptions, and mental health support are not covered expenses in most plans. However, the longer you are a member in good standing, the more goodwill you build up to request that some of these other uncovered expenses be given consideration for coverage.

Monthly dues can range from a low of $125 up to $300 per member, and members are required to pay the first $500 of each health incident before asking the ministry to pay for the balance on covered services. Unlike insurers, most of the ministries are not contracted, so there is no guarantee your bills will get paid. Those willing to participate must trust that the system will be funded when they are in need—there is definitely a "leap of faith" component to it that is not common in the insurance world, where policies are generally assured to be funded and detail exactly what is covered and what is not.

Membership in faith-based cost-sharing plans has exploded since the PPACA became law; individuals belonging to a qualified health-sharing ministry are exempt from paying the fine for not having insurance, as required by the PPACA. According to the Alliance of Health Care Sharing Ministries, more than one million Americans now belong to these organizations, led by membership in Texas and California. There are more than 100 faith-based cost-sharing ministries nationwide, although many of those are small, individual churches and their congregations. As of mid-2017, all of the faith-based sharing ministries in the United States were Christian, but at least one group was nearing completion of organizing a Jewish cost-saving program.

Faith-based cost-sharing programs offer a less expensive alternative for covering personal health costs, with monthly premiums significantly less than what is required in traditional programs. One of the ways faith-based coalitions are able to keep costs down is that most programs do not cover several preventive procedures commonly covered by traditional insurers. For example, colonoscopies, birth control, and mammograms are not generally covered, and members are left to negotiate a cash price and pay out of pocket.

Most of the faith-based programs ask that the member pay the entire fee for each procedure and then request reimbursement. As a result, members must manage personal cash flow consistently, because they will likely have to wait a few weeks after paying the doctor or hospital before being reimbursed by the co-op. Additionally, state or federal regulators have no influence or control over faith-based programs. As a result, if a member has a grievance or is frustrated by a denial, there options for recourse are limited.

VALUE-BASED INSURANCE DESIGN (VBID): Value-based insurance design, commonly known as *VBID*, is exactly what the name describes. VBID models are specialized models incorporating many of the tactics discussed in Consumer Driven Healthcare. VBID models are based primarily on the tactic of charging patients less for high-value or proven clinical procedures and charging more for procedures and treatments that are considered lower value, with less clinical data to confirm their effectiveness.

The highest-value treatment option is not always the lowest-cost treatment option. If a treatment option is much more clinically effective than a less expensive option, it may still be the higher-value option.

Patients can pay a minimal copay or none at all for a procedure determined to be high value, making these procedures more attractive to consumers. Likewise, health plans implement higher cost-sharing responsibilities for patients on procedures and services that have little or no clinical benefit. VBID provides an opportunity for the employer, in partnership with the health plan, to incentivize patients to use high-value, low-cost services with contracted providers.

According to not-for-profit consumer healthcare advocacy group, Families USA, policymakers and insurers should follow eight guidelines when implementing VBID to ensure that consumers have affordable access to high-value care that is best for them:

1. Rely on high-quality clinical evidence.

2. Reduce cost sharing for high-value care and on the contrary, discourage choosing low value providers by increasing cost sharing

3. Have robust networks of high-value providers.

4. Reward providers for delivering healthcare based on clinical evidence.

5. Provide resources that clearly explain the value-based benefit structure.

6. Have an accessible "exceptions process" to allow consumers to get care that fits their conditions.

7. Do not require consumers to participate in wellness programs.

8. Regularly evaluate the plan's benefit design and its effect on access to care.

In summary, VBID is a specialized insurance model that employs consumer-driven healthcare tactics to provide choice to patients when selecting procedures and services. The pricing of these services is often based on clinical outcomes, and choosing one provider over the next can prove to be quite costly. As a result of consumer-driven models like VBID, hospitals will be forced to be more transparent and compete for market share and business in a manner that was not necessary in the past. I like how the *New York Times* summarized VBID, saying it will "nudge patients to do the right thing."

The three programs discussed in this chapter are examples of alternatives to the traditional consumer health plans purchased en masse by employers in America. As companies look to save money and control hyperinflation of healthcare spending, these alternative models have gained significant traction and proven to be a short-term and long-term path to Health-Wealth for corporations.

HEALTH-WEALTH STEP 1: *Investigate and promote alternative health insurance models that complement your company's offerings.*

REDUCE ABSENTEEISM: THE MILLION-DOLLAR PROBLEM

EVERY BUSINESS STRIVES to hire and retain reliable, productive employees. So when your employees miss work days, there is a real cost to your business. Employees missing days are an expense to your company, and this concept is known as *absenteeism*.

There is always a hard cost on your books when your company offers PTO for illness or vacation. But in addition to the measurable expense on your balance sheet incurred from illness-related PTO, there is a less quantifiable but still significant additional burden for absenteeism when that employee is in a revenue-generating role. When those absences become persistent, both your revenue and your expenses are likely suffering, and those losses add up quickly.

Thus, this step will discuss innovative money-saving strategies to reduce health- and dependent-related absenteeism of your most valued employees.

To convert absenteeism to productive work hours, employers must consider and offer a variety of creative and flexible options that may better fit the employee's health and family needs and demands. One example would be specialized programs for your employees with chronic illnesses. This is where a nurse navigator or case manager comes in. Working from home, flex hours and other programs should be considered as well.

One approach to cost containment for these patients is the bundling of high cost and chronic illness services, a tactic employed by companies nationwide that provides negotiated, bulk discounts with local centers of excellence. These bulk discounts don't just benefit the employer through significant savings but also allow steep discounts for the employee for choosing a center of excellence. These bundling programs are not just for specific procedures but for entire episodes of care for a few, specific, high-cost chronic diseases. We will get into greater detail on this bundling option later in Health-Wealth Step 5.

There are several ways to approach excessive employee absenteeism as a result of the employee's poor health or chronic condition. Without self-accountability and a commitment to self-management and a healthy lifestyle, most tactics will be ineffective. This is why converting to a consumer-driven plan is so critical, as without constant reinforcement of personal lifestyle changes, many of these tactics are doomed for failure. Thus, over-communicate and promote these tactics!

Beyond an employee's illness, the main cause of absenteeism, as it relates to your most valued employees, is caring for dependents.

There are three primary categories of dependents who can lead to chronic absenteeism: infants, individuals with special needs, and aging seniors.

When seeking solutions to reduce excessive dependent-related absenteeism, the employer should first conduct a full review of the dependent's benefits. Does the individual or family have insurance, supplemental insurance, gap insurance, veterans benefits, or a convertible life insurance policy? For seniors, beyond just benefits and insurance, a full review of retirement accounts, assets, and other financial options such as a reverse mortgage can be considered as well. Providers have learned through the years that a large percentage of those in need often have access to a benefit that they are not even aware of. It is wise to include the spouse or significant other in this conversation to increase the odds of having all the answers needed to identify any available benefits.

Once you have done a complete benefit and financial review to confirm available financial resources, based on the specific need, conduct a full review of all local, state, and federal programs and associated assistance available for each condition.

It is imperative that these two steps be taken for each employee dealing with dependent-related absenteeism. Determine access to benefits and financial resources, and then identify programs that are appropriate to meet the individual's needs and the associated costs.

Let's pause here to talk further about convertible life insurance. Many policies will allow the insured to cash out the plan in advance to use the funds for long-term care or support in the home. This is one of the best-kept secrets in healthcare, the unknown family benefit. I always encourage individuals to double-check with their life insurance broker before assuming their policy does not include this benefit. Similarly, you may be unaware that the employee's spouse or family member has access to veterans' benefits that could be applied to your employee or dependent. The same goes for employees whose spouse may have supplemental insurance. You never know until you ask, so take time to ask!

Another path to savings on the absenteeism front is a flexible work schedule program. Does your company require a manager on duty after hours or on weekends? You would be surprised how many employees would volunteer to fill those shifts regularly if given the opportunity. This is often times a result of dependent needs and a spouse or partner's work or school schedule. Does your company offer a "4-10s" program for employees to work ten-hour days four days a week and take the fifth day off (usually Friday, but it can be whichever day of the week best meets the employee's need), or offer every other Friday off, or offer a work-from-home option periodically? It's really not that different than those who have weekend military commitments and are on call from time to time. The more flexible the employer is willing to be, the more savings the company can realize.

Many companies have employee assistance programs to assist in funding dependent care and other needs. When the employer offers to pay 20–30 percent of the care needed for a dependent, that can be a significant motivator. Confirm that HSA funds can be attributed to dependent care, as well.

On that note, benefit extension programs are as much a solution as initial benefit support. Benefit extension simply means that finances have run dry on the care that is being provided, and an employee is simply seeking some support to continue providing the home care, assisted living, or other needed service. In fact, benefit extension programs are often better received by employees and family members needing support. They are already well into the care episode and understand the physical, mental, and financial burdens required for each service, so there is often less hassle and fewer unknowns to be figured out as you go.

Many companies have contracted directly with nonmedical home care companies to secure discounted rates and to enhance access for employees, as there is a national shortage of caretakers and no guarantee that a caretaker will be available for the employee's dependent each day. These formalized relationships guarantee the home care company volume, and in return, the employee gets a contracted discount and often even more importantly, they have the peace of mind that a caretaker will be available for their dependent each day.

One of the national leaders in home care, AMADA Senior Care, makes available to each of its care teams a Readmission Prevention certification program. I was part of the nonprofit team that originally created these certification programs, which have proven valuable in preventing unskilled caretakers and family members from unnecessarily sending patients to the hospital and nursing homes when, with the appropriate training and resources, they could have easily remained at home. Preventable readmissions to hospitals and nursing homes can be quite costly to the employee and dependents.

In 2017, for example, AMADA Senior Care's Discharge Admissions Reduction Team Program was recognized nationally as an industry-leading, best practice program in part because it provided a service that most home care companies are not willing to take on. According to Tafa Jefferson, AMADA Senior Care's founder and CEO, AMADA was started on the premise that all patients are cared for just as if they were the caretaker's own mother. As caretakers become more difficult to recruit and retain, it is more imperative than ever that home care companies provide education, resources, and training to all of their caretakers to ensure that each can live up to the company's required level of care. AMADA is among the few home care companies nationwide that have invested heavily in training for caretakers, in spite of very thin profit margins in the nonmedical home care space.

In a personal interview, Jefferson stated that there is really no other way to approach it. "We either provide them the same level of care we would if it were our own mother, or we don't commit to caring for them at all—there is no middle ground."

When seeking a partner to care for employees and their dependents, research the organization's quality history, look into their local history in your market, seek a national brand name when possible, and inquire about enhanced caretaker training programs to ensure they are not sending a completely unskilled caretaker into your employee's home.

When large employers partner with one home care company and guarantee volume or exclusivity in marketing, a care credit program can be created that awards free hours of care to employee dependents when certain benchmarks in both individual and company caretaker hours are achieved. For example, each employee dependent receiving home care support could qualify for five free hours of care per month (paid for by the employer) once seventy-five hours have been paid for each month. The employer can contribute money and ask the home care company to donate a portion of the five hours per month as well—get creative!

Part-time home care support averages about $6,000 a month in the United States, with full-time support ranging from $12,000 to $20,000 a month, depending on the state. The average length of stay for seniors receiving nonmedical home care averages about eighteen months before either funds are depleted, the patient's needs grow too acute and demanding to continue living in a home environment, or they ultimately succumb to poor health and pass away.

Oftentimes, employees and individuals approach home care and long-term care planning from more of a five-year perspective. While that is a smart approach, when considering employee assistance programs, there are many more possibilities when the employer thinks in increments of six, twelve, or eighteen months, potentially capping benefits at eighteen months. By that time, many families have experienced the true value of the services provided and are more willing to deplete savings, dependent funds, or potential inheritance.

In some cases, it may even make sense for the employer to directly contract with one or two caretakers for forty hours a week. These contracted caretakers are allocated exclusively to support your company and conduct brief, daily well-being checks on employees recovering at home from procedures or injuries, as well as their dependents who may need assistance with activities of daily living, including medication adherence, transferring, ambulating, bathing, or eating. This service becomes an extension of your nurse navigator program.

This chapter has discussed a number of proven tactics utilized to accommodate those with chronic illness or dependent needs. Below is a partial list of additional support services to consider for providing relief to employees with dependents in need.

TACTIC	SENIORS	DEVELOPMEN-TALLY DISABLED	INFANTS & CHILDREN
Utilizing the local senior center for midday activities and meals	X	X	
Utilizing a local adult day care for activities and meals	X	X	
Respite care at an assisted living facility, nursing home, or residential board and care facility	X	X	
Contracting with a local church for volunteer support	X	X	X
On-site Uber/Lyft healthcare ride programs	X	X	X
Leverage state-based home care reimbursement programs for families and caretakers	X	X	
Contract with a nurse navigator to manage high-risk or chronically ill dependents	X	X	
Open an on-site clinic and adjacent senior center/adult day care/child day care	X	X	X
Conduct a thorough review with the employee and spouse to identify any extended family benefits	X	X	X
Confirm available community programs and associated costs	X	X	X
Check employee life insurance policies (they may be convertible for end-of-life care support)	X	X	
Employ a liberal, flexible work hour program that meets the needs of your employees	X	X	X
Contribute 20–30 percent of the employee's dependent care costs up to a capped amount each year (dependent spending account)	X	X	X
Contract with a nonmedical home care company for a discounted rate for all employees and dependents	X	X	
Partner with a community nonprofit to create a community/employee assistance program for those in need, and donate tax-deductible dollars to the fund	X	X	X
Create a care credit program in partnership with the nonmedical home care company, based on volume of employee use, that extends additional care at no cost to employees	X	X	
Contract directly with the nonmedical home care company with two individuals to do daily welfare checks on high-risk, high-utilizing dependents at home	X	X	
Provide after-school programs for elementary and middle-school–aged dependents		X	X

Finally, after considering as many of these tactics as make sense for your organization and your community, consider creating a supplemental financial support system as well. For example, several companies have established relationships with not-for-profit entities in which tax-deductible contributions can be made on behalf of community members who need care but do not have the financial resources. In this scenario, your company wins through a tax write-off as well as a reduction in absenteeism and financial savings for the family, if in fact it is an employee who applied for and was granted assistance. This assistance can be in the form of nonmedical home care, medical home care, rent payments for a board and care facility or assisted living, respite care, or simply to install a handrail in someone's house.

As nonprofit community aid organizations evolve, entities are negotiating new support models with long-term care insurance companies that will provide extended episodes of care, which were previously financially unattainable to individuals in need. On top of all this, if you open applications up to anyone in the community, you are now positioning yourself as a good corporate citizen and get a public relation's boost as well. You can ask your board members to get their other companies to donate to the same not-for-profit.

The neat thing about the tactics mentioned above is that each company and each community can pick and choose which of these tactics fits best for them and their population. In fact, employers should consider combining as many of these tactics as possible to reduce absenteeism.

Don't rely on your broker or insurer to bring you solutions. Consider each of the following tactics:

- Eliminate PTO for sick days.

- Create a bonus PTO program for "well days."

- Contract with a nurse navigator to manage high-risk or chronically ill employees.

- Budget for an employee/dependent assistance program.

- Open an on-site clinic and adjacent senior center/adult day care.

- Open an on-site infant and child day care.

- Contract for discounted bundling programs for expensive and chronic diseases (more in Step 5).

- Conduct a thorough review with the employee and spouse to identify any extended family benefits.

- Confirm available community programs and associated costs.

- Check employee life insurance policies. They may be convertible for end-of-life care support.

- Employ a liberal, flexible work hour program that meets the needs of your employees.

- Contribute 20–30 percent of the employee's dependent care costs, up to a capped amount each year.

- Contract with a nonmedical home care company for a discounted rate for all employees and dependents.

- Create a care credit program in partnership with the nonmedical home care company, based on volume of employee use, that extends additional care at no cost to employees.

- Partner with a community nonprofit to create a community/employee assistance program for those in need and donate tax-deductible dollars to the fund.

- Contract directly with the nonmedical home care company with two individuals to do daily welfare checks on high-risk, high-utilizing dependents at home.

HEALTH-WEALTH STEP 2: *Create programs to reduce illness-based and dependent-related absenteeism.*

CONVERT TO DIRECT PRIMARY CARE

ORGANIZATIONS THAT HAVE CONVERTED to a direct primary care (DPC) model have seen an overall reduction in healthcare spending of up to 20 percent.[6] That's significant.

DPC is one of the most rapidly emerging models being employed by large corporations to reduce overall healthcare spending. In addition, DPC is likely to continue gaining momentum for several years to come, as it is proving to save money and enhance customer access and satisfaction.[7]

DPC is a value-based primary care model that increases operational efficiency and doctor-patient satisfaction while reducing overhead by cutting out the middleman, insurance, and all the red tape and bureaucracy from healthcare. In short, DPC medical

---

6   Dave Chase, "On Retainer: Direct Primary Care Practices Bypass Insurance," California Health Care Foundation, April 2013.

7   Ibid.

practices do not accept any form of insurance. Employers and employees are enrolled in an exchange that pays the physician a per-patient monthly retainer fee. This retainer fee most often ranges from $50–$100 a month. In exchange, the individual is entitled to a specified set of services offered by the physician or practice.

How does DPC differ from a concierge practice? Concierge products are more often premium services that are significantly more expensive than $100 a month. Concierge medical practices often accept insurance but also charge a yearly membership for immediate access. Concierge practices are more like VIP or country club medicine, prominent in affluent communities where access to physicians is sparse or long wait times to see a doctor are an issue. This is not the case with the DPC model.

DPC physicians routinely keep a patient panel size of 600 to 800 patients, depending on the region, whereas doctors who take insurance (not including concierge doctors) average closer to 2,500 patients on their panel. As a result, DPC doctors are able to spend quality time averaging thirty minutes or more with their patients, discovering ways to live a healthy lifestyle and optimize one's well-being.

Kat Quinn, a Patient Advocate for MyDPC.org, shares, "One of the best perks about DPC is that many DPC practices offer wellness programs that are included in the membership fee, like yoga, tai chi, nutrition workshops, and more to promote a healthy lifestyle. By offering such value-added services, companies can reduce employee absentee while boosting employee morale and wellness, therefore increasing their bottom line."

Benefits of the DPC model include a stronger patient-doctor relationship, the reestablishing of the personal family physician, and enhanced access to the services offered by the doctor or medical practice. Since you are paying a retainer fee, the doctor has stronger incentives to shorten wait times, improve customer service, and keep patients satisfied. That kind of sounds like the way things used to be, doesn't it?

As a matter of fact, Generation Xers were the first to experience the dissipation of the patient-doctor relationship, as the days of the personal family physician started going by the wayside in the 1970s and 1980s. The 1980s brought an expansion of HMOs, and health insurance largely became reactionary and focused more on catastrophic events. Year over year, the routine, annual health physical became less and less of a priority to American citizens.

Aside from the financial benefits listed below, DPC has already enhanced access to the diminishing availability of primary care in many affected markets. Further, DPC is restoring the accountability of doctors when it comes to fulfilling the needs of their patients, and it reduces the administrative burden of many traditional insurance policies. DPC doctors claim they spend much more time with patients, often advertising up to thirty minutes of direct physician access per appointment. Because each DPC practice's entire book of patients is often smaller than those of practices accepting insurance, doctors have more time for patient interaction and involvement in individual care planning. This additional time spent on care planning allows the physician to better communicate and explain why traditionally routine follow-up tests, exams, and referrals are not needed.

DPC can accomplish several things for your business: enhanced access to primary care, controlled spending on current primary care models, and a drastic reduction in overall spending (when approached properly). DPC doctors minimize ordering unnecessary tests, exams, and specialty referrals and will often only refer patients to specialists who are preferred providers or centers of value that offer a discounted rate for the initial consult. The model actually puts the primary care doctors to work for you, incentivizing them to assist you in reducing unnecessary spending on unnecessary services, which were so often ordered and abused in a FFS model. This additional physician time and access is a critical component of operating a successful DPC model that reduces overall employer healthcare spending.

DPC practices often charge 9–12 percent of the employer's entire healthcare spend. On first blush, this is likely double what your organization currently pays for primary care (most often 5–6 percent). But here is the secret, for many of the reasons listed above and several more, employers who have converted to a DPC model— for the most part—have seen overall spending come down 20–30 percent on average.[8]

This overall savings is a result of DPC practices being incentivized to keep overall spending down and focusing on the following items:

- Reducing unnecessary specialist referrals

- Avoiding ordering unnecessary exams, labs, and medications

- Referring only to specialists and ancillary providers who guarantee a discounted rate for the employer and employee

- Avoiding unnecessary referrals to the emergency department

- Avoiding unnecessary hospital referrals

- Prescribing generic, affordable medications as often as possible

With all this considered, it is important to understand that the employer will essentially be offering two separate insurance policies to each employee; A primary care policy (DPC) and a catastrophic policy (for all else). However, when the overall employer health spend

8   Ibid.

has dropped by as much as 30 percent, the additional administrative headache that comes with managing two separate policies becomes insignificant. Employers converting to a DPC model should also reevaluate the separate insurance offering to ensure they offer a wrap-around policy that covers other needed services and is largely consumer-driven. This wrap-around policy will likely be a high-deductible plan, as the bigger-picture plan here is enhanced trust, transparency, and aligned incentives between the employee, employer, and physician in not ordering unnecessary exams or hospitalizations.

Remember, in the FFS model, doctors were financially incentivized in multiple ways to order exams, tests, hospitalizations, and expensive medications, even when unnecessary. It was almost a "don't ask, don't tell" approach, meaning that the less the doctor finds out about your situation, the more justification he or she has to over-utilize and order unnecessary exams that generate additional revenue for the practice. DPC removes these incentives, which are in direct contrast to the employer's desire to reduce spending on healthcare.

Many of the services in the DPC policy are offered at no cost. For example, the savings on routine tests and wellness checks alone ranges from $35 up to $450 per procedure for the services listed below.

- Twenty-four-hour access to physician or NP

- Allergy injections

- Annual exam

- Annual Pap test

- Chronic care management

- Blood draws

- EKGs

- Flu shots

- Lab tests

- Management of hospital and specialist referrals

- Nebulizer treatments

- Pregnancy tests

- School and youth sports physicals

- Spirometry

- Strep tests

- Urine tests

- Urgent care

- X-rays (imaging)

DPC cuts down employee and employer costs by offering each of these services at no cost to members. Further, although not free, the savings offered on routine lab work and prescriptions can be significant, as illustrated by the following chart.

There are several major insurance carriers that offer paired packages of DPC coverage along with a high-deductible plan for emergencies, niche services, and catastrophic coverage. Their motivation is simple: to retain your business as an employer when you make the decision to convert to a DPC practice while enhancing care and access for your employees.

Kat Quinn believes that DPC is in its infancy. "In the past couple of years, DPC practices have been steadily growing across the nation. I envision by 2020, we will see a DPC doctor in every high-rise and large office building as integrated health and wellness resources for employees. Imagine employees more engaged in their own health and wellness because the DPC perks [incentives] offer more than just primary care."

MEMBER LAB TEST SAVINGS

TEST	MEMBER PRICE	AVERAGE RETAIL PRICE
CBC	$4.00	$50.00
CMP	$5.00	$50.00
Lipids	$5.00	$90.00
PSA	$10.00	$60.00
TSH	$7.00	$95.00
HgbA1C	$5.00	$50.00

Source: Blue Skies Family Medicine

MEMBER PRESCRIPTION SAVINGS

MEDICATION	MEMBER PRICE	RETAIL PHARMACY/ GOODRX COST
Amoxicillin	$1.70	$10.00
Celexa	$1.11	$4.00
Flonase	$8.10	$15.20
Imitrex	$11.59	$20.25
Lipitor	$4.14	$19.00
Metformin	$1.11	$4.00
Singulair	$5.04	$35.00
Z-Pak	$7.82	$15.00

Source: Blue Skies Family Medicine

Quinn adds, "Workplace wellness is the next big trend in employee health and benefits, and at the center, driving down costs, will be DPC."

There is an aligned incentive between the employer and the contracted carrier, as the cost of care to the carrier is no longer a significant when converting from a traditional plan to a dual plan that offers both DPC coverage and a wrap-around plan.

Allow me to financially quantify this opportunity. At present, most companies spend about 5 percent of their total healthcare spending on primary care. By converting to a DPC model, you are more likely to spend in excess of 10 percent on primary care, as you are converting to a subscription model of sorts. With that said, at the end of the month and year, your overall healthcare spend will likely drop by at least 20 percent due to reduced utilization.[9]

The ultimate goal in reading this book is to identify tactics that could be implemented to save your company on its overall healthcare spend. Converting to DPC accomplishes this by spending a higher percentage of its dollars on primary care. In my experience, primary care physicians' decisions can affect up to 90 percent of your overall healthcare spend. So why not align incentives? As a result of this enhanced pipeline to a physician, your employees are often healthier and happier.

The best way to assess your savings potential and the appropriateness of a conversion to a DPC-dual model is to complete the **Health-Wealth Loss Assessment**. However, in comparison to other tactics listed in this book, DPC is one of the easiest, most adaptable, low-cost conversion tactics that has a significant likelihood of saving your organization significant money on overall healthcare spending.

HEALTH-WEALTH STEP 3: *Convert your health insurance offering to a DPC model.*

---

9   Ibid.

CONDUCT AN INDEPENDENT CARRIER AND BROKER EXPENSE REVIEW

YOUR BROKER'S INCENTIVES are not aligned with your goal of saving you every dollar possible.

Let me explain. Before becoming a hospital executive, I operated nursing homes for several years. Shortly after being hired as the administrator of a nursing home in California, I began reviewing our five largest expenses to see if there was opportunity to cut our costs. I noted, of course, that employee benefits were in the top three expenses, so I reached out to our longtime broker, whom I had just met but had worked with my corporate boss for years.

I told the broker I was new and that we needed to cut costs. Since our benefits were up for renewal, I had identified that I needed proposals that would cut healthcare spending by 10 percent. Even though I did not believe he would come back with a full 10 percent savings proposal, I wanted to challenge him so he knew we were serious about this matter.

As luck would have it, he stated that he had just started working with a new carrier that contracted out management to a local third-party administrator, which is very common since the carrier is often based thousands of miles away. Thus, a few weeks later we sat down together, and he showed me that my per-employee, per-month (PEPM) costs would go down significantly with the new carrier, likely 3–7 percent annually. So we switched.

Fast forward one year. Our overall healthcare spending did not decrease. It actually *increased* almost 6 percent year over year. Needless to say, I was not thrilled. So I called our broker and demanded some answers. I had two questions: 1) Did his commission on our account increase as a result of switching to the new carrier? 2) How did he let this happen?

The answer to question one was "Yes," but it took me asking him several times and asking for specifics on his annual commission before he gave me the answer. Question two was more complicated.

He explained that he had experienced a similar unexpected increase with two other clients recently and, after researching the matter, found that even though the carrier's initial proposal offered a PEPM charge that was 10 percent less than the other bids, we were being charged a processing fee for each claim. And to make matters worse, to drive up its revenue, the carrier would separate or unbundle claims for multiple charges and procedures so it could charge a separate processing fee on each.

So I pulled out the proposals from a year earlier and identified in the small print that a claims processing fee would be assessed, but none of the other bids had a processing fee. Had our longtime broker done his job, he would have advised us then that, based on our average annual claims submitted, our costs would be higher with the new carrier and that, as a result, its bid was actually the most expensive bid submitted.

Ouch. This hidden tactic may be new to an executive like me, outside of the insurance industry—but by no means should this have slipped by our broker. I am quite certain it did not slip by, that he was aware of it in advance of the selection, and that he just chose not to disclose it to us, as he saw a significant jump in his personal commission when switching from one carrier to the next. This was a common tactic and business as usual for many years with brokers.

With that story in mind, the goal of this chapter is not to, in any way, suggest that your broker is dishonest and not representing you well. Because the cost of the new approach was volume based, the broker always had an out to say "if we would have had less claims there would have been savings over the prior year." The goal of this book is to arm you with tactics to reduce your healthcare spending, and the only way to truly accomplish that is evaluating your broker along with your carrier. You need an independent review.

Your broker is not independent.

Once you get your arms around that simple truth, you are ready to continue reading this chapter. I can repeat that sentence again for impact, if necessary.

Your broker is not independent.

It's no different than a realtor who represents you buying a new home. The more you spend on your new home, the more your representative gets paid. It's no different with your organization's broker, and there are hundreds of sly and hidden tricks used to hide, insulate, or cover up how a broker's total compensation from each policy is achieved. Buyer beware.

Childhood friend? The boss's cousin? Your broker for twenty-five years? None of these things change a simple fact: No matter how you slice it, your broker will almost always make more money when you pay more.

This tactic is about doing a complete audit or review of every dollar earned by your broker as a result of his or her contract with your organization, as well as every dollar spent on care. While I do not want to over-focus on the broker, the point here is to track every dollar spent, attach it to one of the terms of the broker or carrier agreement, total it all up, and see if there is room for improvement.

Most executives are surprised by at least some portion of the dollar trail. That's the entire point. So Health-Wealth Step Four can be summarized in this manner: Track every dollar spent and look for opportunities to reduce that spending.

A true audit with the needed detail to identify savings opportunities for your organization is far too complex and too large a task for an internal employee to lead. This is not even worth considering. In fact, compare how your company prioritizes the budgeting and management of its healthcare spending in comparison to other top expenditures. The irony is that it is very rare for any organization to have a full-time employee dedicated to managing their second- or third-largest overall expense—healthcare. The 401(k) has its own full-time employed manager, but it's not even in the top five expenditures. Healthcare is often the second-largest expense, behind salaries and wages, and in a few cases is the third-largest expense, behind real estate and lease payments. Why isn't healthcare spending given the same attention?

The point? Contract out to an independent expert who can give you a transparent review of your healthcare spending and where opportunities for savings lie.

When you do contract with a lawyer, auditor, consultant, or independent broker for this service, ask them to sign a disclosure that prohibits them from sharing findings with anyone or referring or suggesting any brokers to you. Realistically, they might help identify some products that you could consider for implementation, but they should stay completely out of recommending an independent broker to you, or the entire mission is flawed.

The only way to truly audit your spending and get a transparent analysis is to hire or contract with an individual who is completely detached and independent from both the broker and the carrier, to provide an unbiased analysis. In fact, the closest most employers ever come to an independent analysis of their carrier is when conducting an RFP. Ironically, those conducting the research, preparing an analysis, and competing for the employer's business by submitting a proposal in response to the RFP are the brokers themselves.

Ultimately, the goal of such RFPs in recent years has been to avoid the annual increase proposed by an employer's existing broker/ carrier team. Hyperinflation in healthcare has been so aggressive in recent years that it's no longer feasible to attempt to reduce your monthly spend to your carrier/broker; a successful annual savings is now viewed as avoiding an increase.

As a result, to win your company's business, competing brokers will often focus on the manner in which your current broker is being compensated as a means of creating the illusion of reduced spending, whether or not it is factual—moving the cheese, if you will. The truth is that, in my experience, the rates offered to brokers by the remaining carriers are often almost identical, and the only means the broker has to offer you savings is by reducing his or her commission. The take-home percentage of commission is often the focus in negotiations, instead of the overall cost to the employer.

The RFP process in itself breeds conformity. It's a flawed, outdated methodology when considering contracting with a health insurance carrier. The very goal of the reevaluation of your broker and carrier is to save on spending by identifying new, different, or more creative approaches to improving employee care without spending more money. Yet the RFP process itself puts significant limits on the participants' ability to be creative or suggest alternative approaches by stating parameters for submission. To make that point event further, the individual designing the RFP, as discussed previously, is the least qualified person in the process to identify RFP guidelines because they are not an expert on the subject. It is a lesser priority in their overall job description that they only allocate time for one every three years.

So, is there anyone available on the free market who is truly independent and could conduct a fair analysis for you? Are benefits advisors truly independent and unbiased? They can be.

While there may be a handful of attorneys or former brokers who offer this type of service nationwide, let the buyer beware. If the benefits advisors is truly independent and advertises such services, remember, this is a capitalistic society, and the sharks will track them down. In this case the sharks are the brokers and the carriers, who have been known to buy lavish dinners and open the doors to their luxury suites to ensure that major accounts come their way. It would be naïve to assume that the same full-court press marketing approach would not be employed on an individual claiming to be an independent broker-carrier auditor.

Whether an organization or an individual, benefit advisors have sprung up in recent years, and many offer the level of integrity and transparency that your company requires. Benefit advisors are an investment worth making. Just research them in advance to ensure they are not just feeding business to friendly brokers!

One of the more prominent examples is the Health Rosetta. The Health Rosetta process is difficult to simplify but involves tactics such as implementing a code of conduct for brokers, a Plan Sponsor Bill of Rights, disclosure forms, and other similar documents. Dave Chase, Founder of the Health Rosetta and a major thought contributor in my preparation of this book, described to me his definition of the Health Rosetta: "The Health Rosetta is a collection of principles and best-practices that serve as a blueprint for examining every expense a company incurs on healthcare delivery and identifying opportunities to reduce costs and improving care."

Dave often compares the current state of healthcare in America to the motion picture *The Big Short*, a movie in which the entire country and its industries ignored all the signs of a financial collapse. His nonprofit, Health Rosetta, was birthed out of a belief that healthcare is bankrupting our country and that at the rate we are going, a minimum of 40 percent—and likely more than 50 percent—of millennials' lifetime earnings will go toward their personal healthcare expenses. That's not only unsustainable and unrealistic; it's insane.

While the **Health-Wealth Loss Assessment** tool will determine whether or not the Health Rosetta is an appropriate fit for your organization, it is just one example in an emerging industry of benefit advisors or independent experts who can conduct an audit of large employers' entire healthcare spend.

HEALTH-WEALTH STEP 4: *Conduct an exhaustive, independent review of every dollar the company spends on its carrier and broker.*

IMPLEMENT DISEASE-SPECIFIC VALUE & CARE MANAGEMENT PROGRAMS

WHAT PERCENTAGE OF YOUR EMPLOYEES account for the majority of your overall healthcare spending? If your company mirrors national averages, then approximately 5 percent of your employees account for more than 50 percent of overall healthcare spending.[10]

Imagine if you could identify that 5 percent and find a way to manage the costs. Well, that's why you bought this book, isn't it? Not only do you have the ability to identify these high-cost employees, but there are now a number of companies nationwide that provide programs to significantly reduce spending on chronic conditions or high-cost services for the employees who account for the majority of your healthcare spending.

---

10   Karen Weintraub and Rachel Zimmerman, "Fixing the 5 Percent," *The Atlantic*, June 29, 2017, https://www.theatlantic.com/health/archive/2017/06/fixing-the-5-percent/532077/.

A recent study noted that 60 percent of American adults have at least one chronic condition, and more than 40 percent have more than one chronic condition.[11] As discussed earlier in the book, an employee's spouse or another dependent with a chronic disease can be just as impactful on the employee's productivity and rate.

Respected, longtime healthcare executive and recently retired Dartmouth-Hitchcock CEO Dr. James Weinstein shared in 2017 that he had identified nine critical ideas for changing healthcare. One of those nine ideas was to focus on the top 5 percent of healthcare users.[12]

As mentioned in Part II, one of the most efficient means of reducing spending is focusing on your high-cost employees and offering disease-specific programs. After first identifying and quantifying the employees accounting for the majority of your spending, identify the chronic diseases and procedures that account for the majority of these dollars. Based on the demographic makeup of your organization and its employees, this is where you have the "a-ha moment." It's likely that several of the following conditions will account for a significant amount of your spending.

Common high-cost diseases, procedures, and surgeries include hip and knee replacement, back surgery, fertility treatment, cancer treatment, and cardiac care. Several complications commonly associated with obesity, including diabetes and bariatric surgery, are also common high-cost services.

---

11 Ayla Ellison, "41% of healthcare spending attributed to 12% of Americans, study finds," *Becker's Hospital Review*, May 30, 2017.

12 Molly Gamble, "Dartmouth-Hitchcock CEO Dr. James Weinstein: 'If we had to redesign healthcare today, it wouldn't look anything like it does now' — 9 ideas for change," *Becker's Hospital Review*, May 23, 2017, https://www.beckershospitalreview.com/hospital-management-administration/dartmouth-hitchcock-ceo-dr-james-weinstein-if-we-had-to-redesign-healthcare-today-it-wouldn-t-look-anything-like-it-does-now-9-ideas-for-change.html.

In recent years, several companies have emerged that are providing specialized programs to employers to drive significant savings. The bundling structures differ slightly, but all have the same goal of reducing healthcare spending while enhancing access and care for a handful of specific, high-costs procedures and complications.

Equity Health, for example, has focused on partnering with large employers to control costs specific to chronic conditions, maternity costs and joint replacement procedures. Equity private labels (A common term for allowing the hospital to brand the program with its own name) specialized disease programs with companies and claims to have the ability to affect up to 75 percent of its overall health-care spend. The Equity model is to identify centers of value in your community and work together to create a full disease-management program, including preventive services, and subsequently negotiate a discount with the provider by offering the likelihood of increased volume.

The Equity model simply takes consumer-driven healthcare to the extreme and ensures transparency from local providers. The employee, or consumer in this model, has access to a website and mobile application that provides information on each hospital that can treat each condition, including pricing, quality, and patient satisfaction data. Most value bundles find creative means to ensure that the value centers are reflected in a much more positive manner on the site or app to ensure that the majority of employees choose the center of value.

Remember, both the employee and employer save significantly when the employee chooses the center of value. In fact, this type of value bundle has proven to be a win-win-win-win: the employee spends less; the employer spends less; the insurer spends less; and the hospital, which ultimately is the source of hyperinflation affecting individuals and businesses, experiences enhanced volume and revenue. Let me provide an example:

Your company completes the **Health-Wealth Loss Assessment** and determines that value bundles are an easy, low-investment, short-turnaround tactic to save significant money. Your data illustrates that 70 percent of employees delivering newborns are choosing to deliver at one high-cost hospital (Hospital A) near company headquarters. Further, more than 50 percent of these employees are having C-sections, often unplanned. Your broker and carrier share with you that obstetrics and newborns are accounting for 12 percent more of your overall spend than for other companies of your size.

Not only is the C-section a riskier procedure, with the potential for very serious complications and health concerns, but it also requires a longer hospital stay and is significantly more expensive than a routine vaginal delivery. Thus, the employer could approach the local hospital and share with them that a change needs to be made. The first option is to allow the hospital to provide the solution by partnering to offer enhanced services for chronic diseases patients, and, of course, a discount. The hospital could put pressure on the then doctors who often recommended the C-section in the first place.

The end result of the conversation is that Hospital A creates a discounted rate for vaginal deliveries, the doctor also discounts services, and the employee is required to pay more for a C-section than a vaginal delivery. The program also includes significant education to patients about the risks of a C-section, as well as the increased copay and patient responsibility if the patient ultimately delivers via C-section.

But what if the Hospital A is unwilling to partner with you?

Well, competition is what makes the value-bundle model work. If Hospital A, the dominant hospital, is unwilling to participate, it's very likely that the other hospital in town, Hospital B, will swing a deal with you that looks significantly more attractive.

So if your employee is in need of a procedure, he or she simply accesses the website or application, compares prices at the various participating hospitals, and sees that there is no employee copay at the preferred hospital, the employee is more likely to choose the preferred partner, and everyone wins. Zero employee copay is much more attractive than having to pay $2,500 or $5,000 out of pocket. The doctor or surgeon performing the procedure could actually be the same doctor at both facilities. You never know until you ask!

This form of value bundle rewards the employee who engages in the process and studies available options. It forces hospitals to price more competitively and be more transparent in disclosing their prices.

A similar but broader approach to identifying savings is often referred to as *specialized wrap-around coverage*. Organizations like Hixme work with employers to offer a variety of health plans and actually allow different family members within an employee's family to enroll in various disease-specific plans. Hixme claims to have "right-fitting" coverage for each individual and also offers partner hospital options and similar ways for employees to utilize centers of value for additional savings.

Employers identify value centers to partner with using multiple data points, but having a strong track record of quality combined with the provider's willingness to negotiate discounted pricing are essential. These programs, even those simply for procedures like joint replacement, are always comprehensive and focus on abatement and chronic care management, not just a short-term episode of care or procedure.

There are several competing entities that partner with employers for more formal disease management programs to rein in spending for your high-cost diseases and procedures. Canary Health offers programs in diabetes management, stress management, and caregiver training. It also offers a self-management program that assists with arthritis, heart disease, and depression.

Livongo is another company that partners with employers and employees to better manage diabetes. Livongo's digital platform is combined with coaching to effectively manage diabetes and keep unnecessary spending down. Omada Health also offers a digital platform that serves as a self-management platform for weight loss, which subsequently reduces risk for type 2 diabetes, stroke, and heart disease. Omada claims its participants lower their diabetes risk by 30 percent and their likelihood for stroke by more than 15 percent. Canary Health, which created a Diabetes Prevention Program and a Chronic Disease Self-Management Program, claims it has reduced diabetes cases by approximately 80 percent, with residual additional savings as a result of reduced emergency department and physician office utilization.

Though much attention is placed on wellness programs and management of chronic diseases like diabetes and heart disease, employers should not neglect the impact of musculoskeletal disorders on their employees. For example, PeerWell, a technology company based in San Francisco, has developed a comprehensive program, PreHab, to aid patients awaiting orthopedic surgery. PreHab is an evidence-based program designed to optimize a person's health profile to the specific surgery they will have. The program offers methods to improve a range of health factors, including exercise, nutrition, social and environment preparation, and anxiety and pain management leading up to surgery. The proprietary PreHab program allows patients to go home faster and perform rehabilitation and recovery from the comfort of their homes, leading to an estimated $2,900 per person in additional savings.

PeerWell's program has become a must-have among patients. Patients from all over the country are proactively seeking out PreHab to improve their surgery experiences and take on more self-care. Employers can do more than they are doing to improve the healthcare experience for their employees struggling with musculoskeletal disorders and can offer solutions to get them back on their feet, feeling pain-free, and able to engage meaningfully in their work.

"Musculoskeletal disorders effect 50 percent of adults and are the leading cause of claims costs by employer-sponsored health plans in the US today," said Manish Shah, CEO of PeerWell. "Much of this cost is driven by surgery, imaging, and prescription medications. In addition, employers need to account for lower productivity, absenteeism, and increased disability and workers compensation insurance premiums. Programs like PeerWell and others can bend the cost curve, improve outcomes, and improve employee satisfaction—all things contributing to employee and employer Health-Wealth."

Separate from disease-specific value programs are modern care management programs like those offered by Quantum Health. Quantum's model is transforming outpatient care management as instead of having one or two nurses responsible for the management of all patients discharging from the hospital, Quantum assigns a care team to a small group of members. That team consists of much more than just one care management nurse. That team includes all specialties involved with the care.

The reason this is transformational, is that traditionally there is one nurse responsible for multiple patients and has to communicate every day with the pharmacists, the lab, imaging, medical supplies, and all other departments. This often leads to significant delays in care and can lead to adverse outcomes as a result. Thus, each morning when the nurse arrives for work and receives the patient's updated status, the nurse begins emailing or calling the other specialists and is unable to authorize additional care until they report back with orders or directives.

Quantum on the other hand has an assigned care team dedicated to a specific group of patients whether they are hospitalized or not. Each morning, they are all present for any updates and can discuss each patient and provide orders in real time. This reduces wasted time and improves outcomes as patients are able to receive care in a timely manner.

These enhanced care management programs are reducing costs by shortening hospital stays, preventing avoidable inpatient days in both the hospital and nursing home, and proactively working with patients to maintain their health.

There are many more programs not mentioned, but there is one common thread in each: the patient must engage in order for both the patient (the employee) and the employer to benefit from these programs. These programs are diverse, have wide-ranging price points, and are not always a great fit based on each company's culture. The time from when an employer first contacts one of these value-bundle providers to the launch of the program within an organization can be just a few short months. However, knowing which company is the best fit for your organization is a critical and complicated first step, as each provider is unique. The **Health-Wealth Loss Assessment** was designed in part to identify which partnerships are the most appropriate fit for each organization.

When it comes to controlling healthcare costs, one of the most effective tactics is quantifying your most expensive patients, identifying common chronic issues and high-cost procedures, and developing specialty programs to more effectively manage these employees. This chapter has shared just a handful of programs available to support you in this process.

In closing, although these bundling approaches may seem laborious and complicated to facilitate, they can actually be one of the simplest and quickest tactics to implement that lead to significant savings. The resources and organizations that manage these programs on your behalf specialize in these services and were created to better care for employees with chronic diseases.

HEALTH-WEALTH STEP 5: *Offer value-bundling benefit programs to better manage high-cost chronic diseases and procedures.*

REWARD LONG-TERM EMPLOYEES WITH FULL GENOME SEQUENCING AND DNA TESTING

IN 2007, GEISINGER HEALTH (now named Geisinger), a large integrated health system in Pennsylvania, announced the launch of a pioneering DNA testing and genome sequencing initiative for the local community that would include any Geisinger patient interested in volunteering. This initiative was a bold move, with financial support from the National Institute of Health and several other health organizations. It was a revolutionary launch in 2007, like none other ever launched in the United States.

Geisinger agreed to pay for exome (partial genome testing) sequencing for all patients who volunteered to be included in the program. At the time of launch, the goal was simply to build a database to learn from, known as a "biobank," and individual results were kept private and not shared with any patients. Genome sequencing is a personal snapshot of an individual and how susceptible he or she may be to chronic diseases, as well as how to best remedy illness through medication consumption or nutritional (food) consumption. You are likely familiar with the term *DNA testing*, and genome sequencing is simply a comprehensive DNA test of an individual. It is as close to personalized medicine as we have come to date. Genome sequencing is essentially a personal road map to improved health that differs from one individual to the next. In recent years, other organizations, including the Department of Veterans Affairs, Kaiser Permanente, Renown Health (Reno, Nevada), and Vanderbilt University, have established similar biobanks that allow them to study the collective data.

Then, in 2013, Geisinger made another bold move by opening up the Geisinger biobank to allow patients to access and learn from their own personal information. Geisinger partnered with a pharmaceutical company, which allowed them to greatly reduce the cost of sequencing. The initiative, called MyCode, has already enrolled more than 170,000 patients, 100,000 of which have already been sequenced, adding approximately 4,000 new members a month. Already, MyCode has identified more than 400 patients with conditions through the program. This is personalized medicine at its finest. It is expected that more than 250,000 individuals will have volunteered and been sequenced by the end of 2018.

"Our approach is *population genetics*. What we're doing—and saying to our friends and neighbors, who are our patients—is, 'Would you allow us to look at your whole genome?' With a 90 percent positive response rate, we've already exceeded our 160,000th full genome, and we think we'll hit 250,000 pretty soon," explained Dr. David Feinberg, Geisinger's president and CEO. At the time the initiative was announced, the cost per individual for sequencing ranged from approximately $1,000–$6,000 per person. Exome sequencing can now cost as little as $300 per person, and full genome sequencing is currently around $1,000 per person, minimum. These costs are for sequencing alone; there are additional costs for analysis.

"We're one of the only organizations taking a population approach to genomics with our MyCode Community Health Initiative. Right now there are definitely some great cancer treatment centers looking at the sub-type of your oncogene and determining medication based on what type of cancer you have. There are definitely tests out there that can look at your genetic profile and determine what medication you should be put on or should be avoided: pharmacogenetics," Feinberg said.

Geisinger works with hospital EMR giants Epic and Cerner. So as long as the patient has a medical record with a medical record number, they can participate in the program. It is likely that hospitals in your community also work with either Epic or Cerner, as they are the two major players in the hospital EMR space and have significant combined market share. This opens the door to you participating in a similar initiative in your community.

"I think it's great what they are doing at Geisinger, how else can you obtain and utilize a person's biological blueprint, as its written in their DNA. And variations in DNA are responsible for the differences in people's appearance, such as having blue eyes versus brown, as well as their physiology, for example being strong versus weak," said Bill Massey, PhD, Associate Professor (University of Arkansas for Medical Sciences), and Clinical Assistant Professor (University of Mississippi Medical Center). "There are so many things we can learn, including an individual's predisposition to disease, and their response to particular medical treatments. Scientists can now read the DNA blueprint of a patient, and based on the known relationships between particular variations in DNA and their impact on biological function, it is possible to predict important aspects of that patient's biology that can be useful in maintaining their health or treating their illnesses."

This start-up cost is the primary reason few companies nationally had ventured down this path. But science and technology had finally progressed to a point that Dr. Feinberg believed that the investment was a no-brainer.

"We're going to prevent heart disease. I think we can say today that if you're a young woman in central or northeast Pennsylvania, your chances of getting breast cancer are lower than anywhere in the world. Because no one is checking entire populations for BRCA and then acting on it. We are. And by doing so it allows us to treat our patients *before* they get sick and helps prevent life-threatening diseases before they take hold. It's changing the course of their lives and the lives of their entire families."

The Center for Disease Control has created a list of tier 1 conditions, and the MyCode initiative, according to the CDC, alerted more than 268 individuals who possessed at least one of these conditions. The tier 1 conditions include the following:

- Hereditary breast and ovarian cancer (early breast, ovarian, prostate, and other cancers)

- Familial hypercholesterolemia (early heart attacks and strokes)

- Lynch syndrome (early colon, uterine, and other cancers)

These are all extremely expensive chronic conditions to treat when employees start experiencing symptoms, and many other screening modalities provide limited detection. These conditions are chronic and become long-term liabilities to an employer.

Dr. Feinberg reported that MyCode also identified ninety-one patients at risk for cardiovascular diseases, including arrhythmia, arrhythmogenic right ventricular cardiomyopathy, Marfan syndrome, and heritable thoracic aortic diseases. An additional thirty-five participants were found to be genetically susceptible to various forms of cancer, and seventeen additional subjects were increased risk for other chronic conditions. Again, these are all expensive diseases to treat.

Without knowing exactly what Geisinger's cost per subject was, let's assume it was approximately $1,000 for the procedure and a follow-up consult with a physician. Hypothetically, assuming all 411 of the conditions identified were from separate individuals and all were Geisinger employees, that total cost of $411,000 is less than one patient's chronic condition can cost in a year to an employer. Now that's ROI! This ROI discussion is hypothetical, but it illustrates the opportunity for improved health and significant Health-Wealth savings.

"So we have this genetic information, along with clinical information, along with 20 years' worth of electronic health records data for four generations of families. And we're returning results to our patients—what is now called precision medicine," Dr. Feinberg added. "But I would say precision medicine is taking care of someone who is already sick. To me, what we're doing is really *anticipatory* medicine. It's coming up with medically actionable conditions and giving that information back to our patients. And no one else is doing that."

Others around the country have ventured into different approaches to DNA testing. The most common area of focus to date has been pharmacogenetics, an emerging science that focuses on each individual's reaction to drugs based on their genetic makeup. Technology has come so far in this area that Medicare began reimbursing for pharmacogenetics-focused DNA testing in 2013.

In a nutshell, a simple cotton swab rubbed on the cheek is sent to the lab and can identify which medications will be effective on an individual and at what dosage. Further, it identifies which medications are not as effective and those that an individual may have an adverse reaction to. Imagine how transformational the results could be if your doctor had a printout of the exact medications your body would react favorably to?

Pharmacogeneticist and neuropharmacologist Dr. Bill Massey is convinced that the financial opportunity for corporate America is significant: "This means healthier employees, fewer work absences, better performance, and a better bottom line for those companies that utilize genetic testing to guide drug selection and health and wellness decisions of their employees. Health insurance companies are only concerned with the *direct medical costs* of treating illnesses (e.g. provider and drug costs). However, the vast majority of the economic impact of employee illness to the employer are *indirect medical costs*, such as absenteeism, lost productivity (even when the employee is not absent), and work quality."

"These variations in DNA allow us to understand why one patient may respond to 'Drug X' and another only responds to 'Drug Y,' even though they have the same disease with the same symptoms," Massey added. "The relationship between genetic variations and different responses to specific drugs is the basis for the new science of pharmacogenetics."

Imagine the savings opportunity if an employee had been taking an expensive medication for years, only to learn that their body was resistant and would more likely react favorably to a much less expensive, generic medication? Or that an employee is actually allergic to a certain expensive medication and that the allergic reaction is the reason an additional medication has been ordered? I could provide example after example.

Knowledge is power, and never is that truer than with genome sequencing.

Geisinger did not focus initially on pharmacogenetics, as so many others were already experimenting with that field. However, Geisinger is starting to spend more time studying the data and how the company may benefit from focusing on pharmacogenetics. And from there, who knows. They are learning so much that it's difficult to predict which direction they will take in coming years.

Although Geisinger has not invested in nutrigenomics to date, that day may come as well. *Nutrigenomics* is a scientific discipline focusing on disease treatment through the study of genes and nutrition. Nutrigenomics is at an even earlier stage on the consumer market than pharmacogenetics, but it can help an individual identify food allergies and potentially harmful antigens in food. Some of the more common findings of DNA testing focused on nutritional consumption are lactose intolerance and gluten intolerance.

Until recently, those suspected of being lactose intolerant or allergic to gluten required a physician visit or blood draw for lab testing. Not anymore. Technology has brought DNA sampling and genome sequencing to the consumer market, and the possibilities of how it might improve individual health seem unlimited.

The top issue is engagement. "We have seen that just knowing your genome leads to improved behaviors. Beyond that, it is about preventing cancer before it starts, and cardiovascular risk," added Dr. Feinberg. "We just look for 'medically actionable,' results and we are learning even more as we go. The benefits seem limitless, but it's been an effective tool in encouraging employee engagement in an even healthier lifestyle now that they have additional resources to rely on."

APPLYING GENOME SEQUENCING IN YOUR ORGANIZATION

Employers should give strong consideration to offering genome sequencing to employees for improved health and as a tactic to reduce employee and employer spending on healthcare. This is actually one of the easier and likely most cost-efficient Health-Wealth tactics to consider.

Make any employee who has been with the organization for more than one year eligible for a free sequencing and follow-up visit with a physician to discuss the findings of the sequence. Models like MyCode have successfully navigated the integrity and privacy concerns that often arise in the early stages of progressive projects that deal with sensitive personal health information.

Geisinger relies on a team of physicians and ethicists for direction. The group has identified employees who are direct relatives but are likely unaware, but that information is kept confidential. Geisinger is finding that employees are not the only ones benefitting from more detail on how to best care for their body. Geisinger itself is learning from the collective body of results, including how trends and warning signs can be more easily identified. The Geisinger process involves a visit with a genetic counselor. Only about 10 percent of the participants need to see an MD geneticist; their care can then be managed by their primary care physician, in most cases.

If one long-term employee is able to identify in advance that they are genetically susceptible to a chronic disease, the ROI from just that employee could outweigh the annual cost for the entire program. The savings could be astronomical.

Naysayers of this Health-Wealth approach often cite two primary concerns: First, that it runs afoul of employee privacy and employee unwillingness to share and desire to protect personal health information from their employer. Second, that by proactively identifying chronic illnesses and areas of concern, an employer is adding to its own cost by now having to allocate resources for prevention and treatment. My answer to number two? Yes, absolutely! That's the whole point of healthcare being an attractive benefit to an employee. Healthcare is a benefit that lets you live healthier and be cared for in times of need.

Employers of all sorts should take the bold move of offering a genome sequencing benefit for long-term employees that includes, at no cost to the employee, testing, a follow-up physician consult, annual physician follow-up, and support services for various concerns and chronic diseases identified in the procedure. The **Health-Wealth Loss Assessment** will also prove beneficial in identifying other critical components each employer should prioritize in their conversion to providing a genome sequencing benefit.

HEALTH-WEALTH STEP 6: *Create a DNA testing and genome sequencing benefit for your employees.*

UTILIZE DATA, ARTIFICIAL INTELLIGENCE, AND MACHINE LEARNING

SEVERAL YEARS AGO, I happened to be speaking at a healthcare event from the same stage as Dr. Tony Slonim, President and CEO of Renown Health in Reno, Nevada. At the time he had just been appointed CEO of an integrated health system in northern Nevada that includes multiple hospitals, physician groups, and health plans. As I listened to him speak, I realized that Dr. Slonim was making some ambitious predictions about the future of healthcare delivery, particularly in northern Nevada. Having lived in northern Nevada for several years, I was intrigued and soaked it in.

After he was finished presenting, Dr. Slonim sat through my presentation, and the two of us ran into each other later in the day and found that we had much in common. Dr. Slonim said to me, "Dr. Luke, your vision is similar to mine, and I am willing to try thin northern Nevada that aren't being done anywhere in America. We are just figuring out where to start!"

Dr. Slonim and I keep in touch, and I have even offered up some support in some of his pioneering efforts at Renown since his arrival. Several years later, in 2017, I was pleased to read about a new initiative that Dr. Slonim had pioneered for Renown, focusing on combining full genome sequencing and artificial intelligence.

Within his first few years in the role, Dr. Slonim partnered with northern Nevada-based Desert Research Institute to find ways to use the Institute's long-standing data on the environment and its impact on the citizens of northern Nevada to improve community health. One of their first steps was contacting the governor's office to request access to social data on Nevada citizens from the Governor's Office of Economic Development. They then partnered with DNA testing company 23andMe.

The result of this project was a voluntary, personalized medicine program designed to improve community health. The first day it was open to the public, the allotted 5,000 slots were all filled, so they immediately expanded the initiative to 10,000 voluntary slots, which also filled quickly. The end result is a program that takes historical data, combines it with modern technology, and utilizes all-new and real-time data to find out as much as possible about an individual in order to identify the best means to care for them and maintain their good health. This is personalized medicine, which is becoming a common theme in achieving Health-Wealth.

Artificial intelligence can be described in many ways, but as it pertains to human health and well-being, it most often describes computer systems that have the ability to identify specific data points and coordinate with other computers or machines and perform various functions in a manner that traditionally required human interaction to complete. As a result, the computers and machines appear to possess intelligence. Think of artificial intelligence as machines searching, reading, learning, and comprehending data, and as a result making suggestions or providing analytical observations without any human interaction or involvement whatsoever.

Northern Nevada's collaboration to improve community health has all the elements to gather data and feed it into computer systems that are designed to perform artificial intelligence, which as a result allows highly specialized, personalized medicine.

As referenced earlier in the book, recently retired Dartmouth-Hitchcock CEO Dr. James Weinstein listed "partnering with industry groups for artificial intelligence and predictive modeling" as one of his nine big ideas to redesign healthcare.[13]

A few examples of machine learning are included below. Although those involved shared the following, they asked us not to include the company name at this time, as the project remains confidential.

> Company A has been experimenting with modifications to their employees' benefit offerings in an attempt to motivate improved health behavior for covered employees and dependents. Company A offered to subsidize the acquisition of wearable technology to monitor activity level, basic physiological readings, and sleep habits. The offering of this option increased employee participation to nearly three times previous uptake levels but also required the employee to allow analytics to be run on their anonymized data. Shortly after starting these analytics, Company A found that it could coach its employees to sleep better by identifying the personal behaviors, such as

---

13   Ibid.

when to exercise, affecting better sleep sessions. There may have been no direct causation, but there was a recognized improvement in overall health statistics for those employees who followed the guidance.

Another confidential example of artificial intelligence and machine learning is from a healthcare provider in an area affected by inversion layers, which create pollution leading to environmentally exacerbated breathing conditions. The provider was challenged to effectively target which emergency care units needed additional or reduced staffing based on the daily conditions. The search for information sources to guide these decisions began with mining geo-tagged social media feeds (e.g., Twitter) for certain terms and phrases to identify prospective "hot sites." Interestingly, as the basic model was refined, the health system started to get up to a four-hour head start on staffing requirements at their various facilities. The more data that machine learning or artificial intelligence engines can ingest, the greater guidance and recommendations can be provided.

This approach was further augmented by having access to fully consented asthma registries, allowing for more understanding of where the provider's most affected patients might be. This moved the model from staffing to an early warning method for those on the registry. The health system is now looking to do more of a crowd-sourcing model by issuing GPS-enabled inhalers and identifying areas where the inhalers are being most used. This approach not only saves the health system money but also improves health outcomes for all involved.

Another pioneering story comes from Fullerton Health in Singapore which operates in collaboration with KenSci, a Seattle-based machine learning company for healthcare. Fullerton Health provides corporate healthcare and third-party administration of care for over 9 million people across 25,000 employers in Asia. In early 2017, teamed up with KenSci to predict who might get sick, how and when comorbidities might develop, and to predict cost of care.

They discovered that 10 percent of the covered lives were consuming 70 percent of the resources due to chronic conditions. The client implemented machine learning solutions to predict and identify the likelihood of chronic disease development and progression among individual employees. By identifying potential future high-utilizers of healthcare dollars with the use of prescriptive analytics, Fullerton Health could tailor processes for this employer to include better care pathways, resulting in improved care for employees with chronic conditions. Fullerton Health's Chronic Disease Management program for corporate employees helped this customer decrease employee absenteeism while reducing costs for managing the health by 60 percent in one year.

How might a private employer benefit from machine learning? The possibilities are limitless if individual employees are willing to allow access to personal health information and proactively contribute to the process. Numerous successful implementations like those at Fullerton Health and Renown Health, although Renown's program is still in its infancy, have shown that it not only brings down cost of care but also provides individuals with early warning and predictions about life-threatening diseases.

As it relates to employers directly, there are organizations offering consumer-centric machine learning programs. One industry leader, Betterpath, describes its platform as "harmonizing disparate healthcare activities simply by getting all of one's patient data in one place. It aligns past, present, and future data in an integrated record designed to provide patients, their caregivers, and their providers with information to manage and optimize care decisions." The data continues to accumulate over time to help identify personalized, outcomes-based interventions.

Betterpath partners with self-insured organizations and seeks out patient recaps and data from hospitals, home care agencies, long-term care facilities, physicians, and health plans to accumulate a comprehensive data set. Once the baseline data is accumulated, patient and caregiver contributions are added in real time, as is any additional pertinent data that may be useful and is contributed by the individual, family member, caregiver, or clinician. This database is accessible online and via mobile application to all parties given permission to access it, which may include family member, clinicians, doctors, or caretakers.

The benefit of employer-sponsored artificial intelligence initiatives is that larger employers have the ability to pressure local hospitals and medical groups to participate out of fear of losing business. When an employer approaches a hospital, health plan, or medical group about data sharing to improve health there is significant incentive for hospitals, health plans, and doctors to participate.

In summary, Health-Wealth Step 7 is a recommendation that an employer proactively create a voluntary artificial intelligence and machine learning program for its employees. All employees within the company are eligible to participate, offered access to the online portal and mobile application, and encouraged to proactively contribute and add to their personal file as often as possible. The more information, the better. Even if on the surface it may not seem relevant to improved health, information should still be input.

The program also includes a free annual consult with a physician or NP—only after the employee has provided the background and historical data required to begin the program, however. The specific data each employer might ask for to initiate the program will differ, but once this initial step is complete and the employee is actively engaged, artificial intelligence and machine learning in a broad sense is the most efficient path to truly personalized medicine that eventually will eliminate a significant amount of unnecessarily healthcare spending.

HEALTH-WEALTH STEP 7: *Identify community partners to utilize artificial intelligence and machine learning to improve employee health.*

PROMOTE TELEHEALTH AND REMOTE MONITORING SERVICES

I WAS SERVING as the event executive chair and emcee for the World Congress on Hospital Readmission Prevention in 2014 in Orlando, Florida. That same day, the event promoter was cohosting a separate event in the room next door, titled World Congress on Telehealth & Remote Monitoring. For the closing session, the two groups were combined, and I was asked along with the executive chair of the other event to deliver a closing keynote address to the combined crowd.

I presented first and was pleased with my delivery as I wrapped up and sat down. As is the norm, a crowd of people in the audience came to ask questions and exchange business cards when I exited the stage. However, out of courtesy for the other presentation, I let everyone know that I would answer as many questions as desired once my colleague was finished delivering her closing keynote. I was confident that my presentation would be the better of the two, as I had been getting consistently positive audience feedback at recent events as an up-and-coming public speaker.

As I sat down in the crowd to hear her presentation, I thought it was odd that she was carrying a laptop onto the stage, walking slowly, and taking her time, as the technical team usually has the laptop ready to go. As she plugged in the laptop and logged on, she did not acknowledge the crowd. This dragged on for more than two minutes and became an almost uncomfortable silence. Before she even spoke, I was thinking to myself, "I am going to steal the show and be the best closing keynote, no way she can hang with me based on what I have seen so far!"

Seconds later, onto her screen popped a video image of a man and a young boy. A few seconds later, the dark-skinned man said hello to the presenter in broken English, and she continued the conversation with him via her computer. She still had not addressed the crowd when she asked if she could examine the ear of the young boy next to him. The man on the screen grabbed the medical device used to examine the inner ear, gently placed it into the boy's ear, and there it was for the entire audience to see … a video image of the boy's inner ear, just as you would see in a doctor's office.

"Looks good," she said. "Now let me look at his throat please. How is he feeling?"

The man set down the ear device, picked up another device, and placed it in the young boy's mouth. The entire audience then viewed the boy's throat. "He is feeling much better now, thank you," the man responded.

"Can you tell us the name of your clinic and where it's located," she said.

"Good Samaritan Clinic in Guatemala City, Guatemala," he replied.

A gasp was heard throughout the room when he said that. And I knew I had lost. Before she had even started presenting or made eye contact with the audience, she had slain me. Her presentation was already more impactful. Wow, I thought, that's an effective approach to communicating the capabilities of modern day medicine when telehealth and remote monitoring capabilities are applied. Impressive.

While this is just one example of applying technology to improve care delivery, what we witnessed was not much more than the use of Skype and a few common medical device cameras. Yet we were all blown away. And this was in 2014! Why? We all used similar technology daily, but few organizations had applied it to care delivery at the time.

A lot has changed in the short years since then. Technology has improved the speed and efficiency at which healthcare is delivered at a rapid pace in multiple ways. Nowhere is that more present than with the adoption of telehealth and remote monitoring capabilities.

Corporations throughout the country have realized that by providing a health plan that allows and encourages the use of telehealth appointments and remote monitoring capabilities can reduce costs significantly and reduce employee loss time.

Once your corporate health plan allows and promotes remote physician consults, providing a private area within your office building that is wired for remote visits is a cost-efficient way to encourage the growth of remote consults. This is the exact manner in which residents of island communities or rural areas have been conducting virtual consults for years.

A number of corporations provide mobile applications that allow the patient and doctor to communicate through video on personal mobile phones or tablets. Some employees would prefer more privacy than simply using the phone out in an open area, and this serves as incentive for the employer to create a quiet, private area for employees to participate in virtual consults.

There are services that ensure a physician or NP is available at all times, appointments can be scheduled electronically, and "walk-in" time slots are often guaranteed for immediate access to a clinician who can remotely inspect the patient through video monitoring and discuss the issues with the patient as well.

The rapid adoption of telehealth consults is one of the major drivers of the significantly reduced employer and employee spending reported by many companies that have converted to consumer-driven healthcare plans.

Similarly, remote monitoring devices are being deployed routinely for a number of common chronic diseases, as well as other health needs. Seniors battling congestive heart failure are often provided a Bluetooth scale, as sudden weight loss or gain can be an early indication of complications, so when they weigh in every day, the result is electrically reported; if there is a significant loss or gain, the patient's insurer, physicians, or clinical case manager is automatically notified. Other examples of remote monitors are devices that simply monitor heart rate, or devices that send an alert each time a patient stands up or sits down. The capabilities of remote devices in improving care are endless.

Further, as employers address chronic disease through value bundles and other coordinated programs, remote monitoring devices are almost always one of the tactics included in the care plan. The cost of many of these devices has come down significantly. At least seven of the nine steps to Health-Wealth in some manner include a component of telehealth or remote monitoring. This illustrates how beneficial this approach can be in reducing wasteful spending on healthcare.

In summary, employers should consider a health plan that allows and promotes remote and virtual visits, provide mobile applications and private, on-site rooms to enhance access, offer no-copay or reduced copay if employees conduct a virtual visit as opposed to one in person, and provide remote monitoring devices for patients with chronic diseases.

HEALTH-WEALTH STEP 8: *Make your organization friendly to telehealth and remote monitoring.*

EDUCATE AND CELEBRATE INTEGRATIVE MEDICINE

THE NINTH STEP to Health-Wealth is to allocate $250 for each employee to have a one-time naturopathic and integrative medicine consult. Why not? Isn't that how medicine was practiced before Big Pharma squashed it? Yes, as a matter of fact, in many ways it was.

I remember first reading about the gluten-free craze around 2010 and being skeptical. Then a good friend mentioned that converting to gluten-free foods was the only thing that has resulted in a noticeable difference in the consistently erratic behavior of his seven-year-old son, who has Down syndrome. But due to his inability to communicate in the manner that other youth his age would, it raised my awareness that the observations of his parents and physicians were critical.

Then, after accepting my fourth and final position as a hospital CEO, I met a young lady at our corporate office who, by coincidence, grew up in my home town, forty miles away from downtown Los Angeles. She was actually my boss's executive assistant, and one day when she ordered the continental breakfast for our weekly CEO meeting, she mentioned that she had gone gluten-free two years earlier. I kind of chuckled when she said that, and I am pretty sure I offended her. She turned, looked at me sternly, and said, "I was on my deathbed for almost four years, and within days of going gluten-free I started feeling healthier and discontinued my meds within weeks and felt better than I had in years."

While this chapter is not about going gluten-free, it is about considering the root cause of disease and illness instead of always focusing on the effect. And when the employer buys in, it increases the likelihood that the employee buys in. The end result can be thousands of dollars in Health-Wealth savings!

Are you aware that most physicians do not receive any training on nutrition in medical school? Does that concern you? If not personally, does it concern you that you are the individual within your organization who is financially responsible for the health and financial well-being of your entire workforce and that their doctors are not trained to discuss nutritional issues with them? It should. Most doctors claim that it's not their responsibility to discuss nutrition with you, that there are other specialists for that. Integrative medicine encompasses the use of a nutritionist to ensure your body is being fed an optimal diet based on your DNA and historical reaction to individual foods and ingredients.

Many people liken integrative medicine to what we commonly refer to as "wellness" in America, which is often associated with Eastern medicine practices. I prefer the term "healthy lifestyles" as opposed to "wellness," as it combines wellness tactics with personal engagement in making wise eating and exercise habits. Integrative medicine addresses the whole person, including mind, body, spirit, emotion, and lifestyle. Some often associate it with naturopathic or holistic medicine. But integrative medicine is actually all those things combined—naturopathic approaches combined with modern, Western medicine practices.

Integrative medicine approaches focus on identifying the root cause of the issue, instead of just focusing on symptoms. One of the primary goals is to prevent additional, often more serious symptoms from occurring. Kyle Hill, CEO of integrative medicine company Harvey, describes integrative medicine in this manner:

> When you combine *Eastern Medicine* philosophies such as nutrition, prevention, and natural self-healing with advanced, evidence-based lab testing of Western medicine, you get a new form of medicine called *Integrative Medicine.* Integrative doctors view symptoms as warning signs of nutritional deficiencies in the body, environmental toxins, improper body functioning, or unfavorable lifestyle habits. They help patients find the root cause of chronic health conditions and focus on treating the whole person, not just a set of symptoms in perpetuity.

Let's be clear here. There are a lot of people out there claiming to be naturopaths or homeopaths pushing natural approaches who are not physicians and unfortunately end up casting much doubt on the naturopathic medicine approach. These folks are not doctors; they are simply selling a product and trying to make a living. That's not what we are talking about here.

We are referring to medical doctors trained to study the root cause and take a comprehensive approach, not simply write a prescription for a medication that does not always address the problem.

So let's define *integrative medicine*: Integrative medicine uses natural (unprocessed) health and wellness approaches to address the root cause of disease, often trying to eliminate that root cause instead of simply focusing on treating the symptoms. Integrative approaches complement but do not replace more mainstream remedies, often referred to as "Western medicine" approaches.

So let's define *naturopathic medicine*. The American Association of Naturopathic Physicians defines naturopathic medicine as: a distinct primary health care profession, emphasizing prevention, treatment, and optimal health through the use of therapeutic methods and substances that encourage individuals' inherent self-healing process. The practice of naturopathic medicine includes modern and traditional, scientific, and empirical methods.[14]

Integrative medicine sounds a lot like naturopathic medicine, does it not? Well, it's very similar, but integrative medicine is more comprehensive and combines *naturopathic medicine* with additional approaches.

Americans' access to sweets, artificially flavored foods, and diet sodas containing scientifically created chemicals that often act as a sweetening replacement for sugar are prime examples of the lifestyle changes in recent years with unknown outcomes—not to mention the growth in popularity of greasy, fatty, and processed foods. These factors have all likely led to an entire new set of diseases and symptoms unfamiliar to prior generations.

---

14 "Definition of Naturopathic Medicine," American Association of Naturopathic Physicians, n.d., http://www.naturopathic.org/content.asp?contentid=59.

The need for expansion of integrative medicine is largely because, in my experience, pharmaceuticals have been largely ineffective in treating many of these newer symptoms and diseases that are becoming more common in American society. I believe there is little evidence that drugs can prevent all chronic diseases but in most cases just provide a temporary fix or pain relief.

Most major insurance companies do not cover integrative medicine services. It lacks logic that major insurers have moved away from covering the root cause of disease, but based on my research, when studying the history of integrative medicine, it becomes clear that Big Pharma used its massive budget influence to push integrative medicine into the background in the 1950s. Big Pharma wanted to the world to believe that drugs can cure all diseases, and they were successful in establishing that as a core belief globally. Money talks, does it not?

As a result, Americans quit focusing on natural approaches and relied on drugs to make them feel better. Because in most cases drugs provide at least a short-term fix, this approach became mainstream and naturopathic doctors and schools declined significantly in the 1960s and 1970s.

Nowadays, the majority of the top twenty hospitals nationwide have opened up some type of integrative medicine practice. One of the many benefits of integrative medicine is that it is often a cash pay model, which allows the doctor to spend more time with the patient. This increased face time with doctors, whether remotely or in person, is a common theme in several of the nine Health-Wealth Steps. Maybe there is something to it?

As millennials become more influential and economically stable, primary medical practices around the country are implementing integrative approaches and hiring integrative medicine doctors. The millennials demand it. This is how they were raised: to live healthy and take care of their bodies. As a result, there has been explosive growth in the practice of integrative medicine since 2000, after fifty years of it being pushed into the background. Those with chronic diseases often figured out that Big Pharma had no cure or that it was too expensive to access, so they sought alternative approaches.

Integrative medicine supports a movement away from generic drug store vitamins and emphasizes specialized natural approaches. In the case of vitamins and supplements, this means conducting lab tests to see which vitamins and supplements can best meet the needs of your biological makeup. Refer back to the chapter on whole genome sequencing to learn more. Integrative medicine is another example of employers investing in better understanding each individual's body and how to best address each body's specific needs.

My research on integrative medicine showed that there are several companies making a difference in the space, most notably tech start-up Harvey, which has taken a comprehensive integrative medicine approach, implementing full-scale telehealth, remote monitoring, and home-based lab services to ensure a low-cost model for patients. Harvey, named after William Harvey, the English doctor who first discovered how blood circulates, was created to help those with chronic conditions optimize their health. Harvey offers home-based consultations with functional and integrative doctors, uses home-based lab testing and procedures combined with telehealth and remote monitoring capabilities to provide natural treatments and solutions, and accomplishes this in a manner that's much cheaper than other companies who have offered integrative medicine as more of a high-cost, concierge-type service.

As the Nine Steps to Corporate Health-Wealth were written, it did not go unnoticed that integrative medicine is a comprehensive approach that utilizes several of the Health-Wealth Steps to improve health and reduce spending for the employer and employee. In a sense, integrative medicine brings many of the recommended steps to Health-Wealth together into one coordinated program.

Not all companies in the integrative medicine space are necessarily viewed as integrative medicine providers. For example, companies like 23AndMe and Helix are more focused on DNA testing and mapping your genetic data. Helix states the following on its website:

> We read your DNA using true next-generation sequencing, which unlocks 100X more data than other companies. Where they do single tests, we assemble, store, and protect your genetic data so you can access and share it with any partner of your choosing without ever having to provide another saliva sample.

Helix offers food, supplements, and wellness products, and each is associated with different gene types and recommend for individuals once they identify their genetic map.

Color, found online at Color.com, boasts that its service helps individuals better understand their risk for hereditary cancers and also focuses on those susceptible to hereditary high cholesterol. Although Helix focuses more on product sales, Color approaches employee health by developing an overall wellness plan to address the findings using multiple treatment plans and approaches. Color has a specific product offering developed specifically to support corporate human resources departments.

Another well-known company in the space is uBiome, which claims to be the leading microbial genomics company. Its website states the following:

> The human gut is home to trillions of microorganisms, which are collectively known as the microbiome. These microbes play

a vital part in our gut health, supporting digestion and the synthesis of vitamins.

A lot can be learned from the human gut, but that's not what this chapter is about. This chapter is about combining multiple approaches of naturopathic medicine with machine learning and DNA testing. The end result is a road map to healthier food consumption, supplements, and more effective drug regimens based on an individual's genetic makeup. That is comprehensive integrated medicine, and if your company invests in it, it's a direct path to Health-Wealth.

In September 2017, another sign of the reemergence of integrative medicine was when the University of California, Irvine received a $200 million donation to launch a new health program to promote integrative medicine. The leaders behind the initiative, Howard Federoff, MD, PhD, and CEO of UC Irvine's health system, and Shaista Malik, MD, the director of UC Irvine's Center for Integrative Medicine, state that other medical schools are too slow to adopt alternative therapies that reveal promise in clinical trials and suggest it is time to transform healthcare to focus on a patient's full range of needs rather than just treating an illness.[15]

So, after learning about a handful of national providers in the space, some very focused on one component of naturopathic and holistic medicine and others providing a more comprehensive approach, it is clear that by encouraging your employees to go down the path of integrated medicine, there is significant Health-Wealth

---

15 Alia Paavola, "$200M donation to UC Irvine for alternative therapy meets criticism," *Becker's Hospital Report*, September 20, 2017, https://www.beckershospitalreview.com/finance/200m-donation-to-uc-irvine-for-alternative-therapy-meets-criticism.html.

opportunity, resulting in improved health and significant savings for employers and employees.

HEALTH-WEALTH STEP 9: *Provide each employee with an integrative medicine consult and healthy living plan.*

SOCKS WITH SANDALS

IT WAS NOVEMBER 2014, and I was delivering my first-ever international keynote presentation. More than 300 executives from around the world, mostly from Central and South America, had come to hear me speak on how to control healthcare costs. I stood on the stage at the Trump International Hotel in Panama City, Panama, ready to reel off my typical opening joke that always made the crowd laugh.

"I like to open my presentation with this PowerPoint slide for two reasons," I said with an anticipatory smile, preparing for the audience to respond to my next line with laughter, as was the norm. The slide listed a summary of my recent work history. "Not only does this opening slide show you my diverse professional background, but it also shows you that I can't keep a job for very long!" I said with a smile as I let out a loud chuckle.

Uh oh ... No one else was laughing. A long, uncomfortable silence filled the room.

The crowd always loves that joke, I thought to myself. What went wrong? Was my delivery off? Did I butcher the punch line? I did a quick analysis in my head and realized where I miscalculated: The entire audience spoke another language. English was their second language. The joke was lost in translation, and there was no turning back. I bombed it.

I rarely get nervous or sweat on stage, but within seconds, I felt both overcome my body.

Quick, I thought to myself, get to the slide with the cute picture of my grandmother and tell the story of how I gave up private jets and celebrity sports marketing as a career to manage nursing homes. That always draws the crowd in.

But wait, I have three or four other sure-fire jokes later in my presentation as well. Will those bomb too? Will the crowd think it's funny in a few minutes when I emerge from behind the podium with my shoes off, with only a single leather strap of Birkenstock sandals over my red, polka-dot socks, so I can illustrate the contrasts between Gen Xers like me and millennials who think that socks with sandals are totally uncool?

The nerves were running high. So what did I do. I tried one more of my surefire one-liners. And it bombed as well.

So I pivoted. I pivoted to material that was not likely to get lost in translation. I stuck to the facts on how to manage company expenses to keep healthcare from bankrupting a business. No more jokes, no more one-liners. Just the material. As the presentation evolved, with each of the remaining forty minutes, I saw the crowd become more engaged. Their posture improved, their facial expressions illustrated their interest, and I regained my confidence. I pivoted, and it worked. I was willing to try something new—avoid the humor and stick to the reason they came. They came to hear me speak because I am an expert sharing proven theories and experiences that can help them. Forget humor, let's give them what they came for, I thought to myself as I proceeded.

That calculated pivot paid off for me. I finished strong and got several topical audience questions as I wrapped up my presentation. Individuals lined up to meet and greet me when I was finished as well, and the event host advised me later that there was so much interest at the table outside the door that they sold out of copies of my most recent book, *Ex-Acute: A Former Hospital CEO Tells All on What's Wrong with American Healthcare*. A few weeks later, my audience feedback results came in very strong, and the event host subsequently hired me to present at several more events in coming years.

Since then I have presented internationally in several other countries and always recall that my usual jokes and one-liners are a slippery slope. I still try my jokes in places like China and Germany, and audience responses can be hit and miss, but I won't be caught off guard again like I was in Panama!

You were hired to be a financial steward for your company. You have the power and influence to pioneer this momentous turnabout for your company. This book represents your opportunity to pivot in the best interest of your organization. The fact is that this decision and action plan are long overdue. But to date, no one has provided a road map on how to pivot—until now. You know have the roadmap, tools, and confidence to lead this change. Do you have the courage to lead this bold but necessary transformation?

Health-Wealth is your road map. And now that you have read the problem (Part I), identified that consumer-driven care and a Health-Wealth culture are essential (Part II), and learned about nine tactics to consider (Part III), the next step is to complete the online **Health-Wealth Loss Assessment**. The assessment is a tool created to do a Strengths, Weaknesses, Opportunities, Threats (SWOT) analysis specific to corporate healthcare spending. It was created to help identify where the biggest opportunity lies for a company ready to take back control of one of its top three expense line items and manage Health-Wealth just like any other critical expense in the business.

Health-Wealth: The correlation between hyperinflating healthcare costs and your company's declining net worth. Today your organization starts bending the curve back to achieve both improved health and increased wealth. And it starts with you. You are the champion who leads the pivot … even if you too think that wearing socks with sandals is uncool and for goofy old men.

WHY HEALTH-WEALTH
IS SO PERSONAL TO ME

IN 1998, I WAS LIVING my dream. I was a newlywed, and I was hanging out at Dodger Stadium almost nightly, as my older brother Matt had made the major leagues and was handling baseball slugger Mark McGwire's sports marketing efforts as he chased down Lou Gehrig's home run record. But then, in 1999, frustration over the lack of communication between my grandmother's caretakers and the desire to find a career path that would prove more fulfilling launched my journey to a new career in healthcare. I became a healthcare administrator with the goal of putting my own fingerprint on care delivery in America.

And then in 2010, there were two major events that affected my life. First, my mother was diagnosed at age sixty-five with Alzheimer's disease. And that same year, as I was serving my fifth year in the role of hospital CEO, President Obama passed his landmark healthcare legislation, commonly known as Obamacare.

It wasn't until almost five years later that the irony of those two events happening in the same year struck me. On January 6 of 2015, I learned that my mother, who taught me to read as an toddler was no longer able to read herself as a result of her progressing Alzheimer's disease. I was angry. I was sad. And I was filled with conviction.

In the same moment, I learned that my mother had lost her ability to read, I was overcome with guilt that I had lost sight of the very reason I entered healthcare fifteen years earlier. Poor communication and a lack of focus on patient's needs brought me to a career in healthcare. And now, fifteen years later, I was overwhelmed by the realization that I was now part of the problem. I was a healthcare leader in a broken system, focused solely on capitalism and not on the patients we have committed to serve. I was as guilty as being motivated by "following the dollar" as every other hospital, doctor, and provider. The patient was no longer my priority; I had become part of the machine that is the American healthcare delivery system.

So when ForbesBooks reached out to me in search of an author to pen a book on healthcare affordability in America, they proposed a simple question to me: Have American businesses and families reached the Health-Wealth tipping point on their ability to afford basic healthcare services?

My first thought was the predicament my wife and I were forced into in 2011 when I lost my job. The monthly health insurance premium for my family of five exceeded $1,500 month, and my wife and I made the decision to go without insurance, because even after seven years with a six-figure income, we could not justify the monthly expense.

That was our Health-Wealth tipping point. And we pushed back. We took a chance. It was scary. We went without for several months until I started a new job. Other American families and businesses are reaching their Health-Wealth tipping point every day.

This is why Health-Wealth is personal to me. I have lived it. I see American businesses closing and families going broke as a result of an industry out of control. If I was not able to afford healthcare for a few months after earning a six-figure income for more than seven years, then what percentage of Americans could?

We've reached our Health-Wealth tipping point in America, and what's right is right. It's time to take a stand. I have been blessed with the tools and experience to lead the charge to Health-Wealth in America.

This is why Health-Wealth is personal to me.

HEALTH-WEALTH STEP 1: *Investigate and promote alternative health insurance models that complement your company's offerings.*

HEALTH-WEALTH STEP 2: *Create programs to reduce illness-based and dependent-related absenteeism.*

HEALTH-WEALTH STEP 3: *Convert your health insurance offering to a DPC model.*

HEALTH-WEALTH STEP 4: *Conduct an exhaustive independent review of every dollar the company spends on its carrier and broker.*

HEALTH-WEALTH STEP 5: *Offer value-bundling benefit programs to better manage high-cost chronic diseases and procedures.*

HEALTH-WEALTH STEP 6: *Create a DNA testing and genome sequencing benefit for your employees.*

HEALTH-WEALTH STEP 7: *Identify community partners to utilize artificial intelligence and machine learning to improve employee health.*

HEALTH-WEALTH STEP 8: *Make your organization friendly to telehealth and remote monitoring.*

HEALTH-WEALTH STEP 9: *Provide each employee with a complimentary integrative medicine consult and healthy living plan.*

THE HEALTH-WEALTH
LOSS ASSESSMENT

This page includes a few questions that serve as a sample of the online Health-Wealth Loss Assessment. For the complete online assessment visit **Health-Wealth.com/Loss Assessement**.

This tool assesses how much money your company is likely to save and which steps are most appropriate for your company. The following assessment will assist you in determining your organization's financial waste on healthcare spending as well as which steps to Health-Wealth are most likely to reduce your company's overall spending on healthcare. It will only take a few minutes of your time; let's get started.

1. Most organizations list their top three expenditures as labor, benefits (healthcare), and real estate/rent. How would you rank healthcare in terms of your largest expenses?
   a. Healthcare & benefits are our largest expense
   b. Healthcare & benefits are our second-largest expense
   c. Healthcare & benefits are our third-largest expense
   d. Other: Healthcare & benefits are not in our top three expense line items

2. My company's health plan is:
   a. Self-insured
   b. Fully insured

3. The following best describes my company's healthcare offerings:
   a. A traditional employer-driven plan only
   b. A high-deductible, consumer-driven plan only
   c. Both a traditional employer-driven plan and a high-deductible, consumer-driven plan
   d. Both a traditional employer-driven plan and a high-deductible, consumer-driven plan with intentional employee engagement

4. The following best describes our corporate culture as it relates to heath and healthcare:
   a. Issues related to employee health and lifestyle are private to the employee.
   b. The company offers information and resources for healthy living to employees on a voluntary basis.
   c. Employees are educated and empowered to pursue wellness through healthy living plans that are actively measured and supported by the company.
   d. Promoting health is an organizational core value, embedded into the culture with many tactics, including formal health-related financial incentives for employees.

5. Does your company have any programs catering to employees with chronic diseases?
   a. Yes
   b. No
   c. Yes, but very low utilization

To take the full, free Health-Wealth Loss assessment and receive your personalized feedback, visit: **Health-Wealth.com/Loss-Assessment**.

A Special Offer from ForbesBooks

Other publications bring you business news. Subscribing to *Forbes* magazine brings you business knowledge and inspiration you can use to make your mark.

- Insights into important business, financial and social trends
- Profiles of companies and people transforming the business world
- Analysis of game-changing sectors like energy, technology and health care
- Strategies of high-performing entrepreneurs

Your future is in our pages.

To see your discount and subscribe go to Forbesmagazine.com/bookoffer.

Forbes